A Gift for

Presented by

I DARE SAY

I DARE SAY

Inside Stories of the World's Most Powerful Speeches

Ferdie Addis

The Reader's Digest Association, Inc.
New York, NY / Montreal

A READER'S DIGEST BOOK

First published in Great Britain by Michael O'Mara Books Limited,
9 Lion Yard, Tremadoc Road, London SW4 7NQ

U.S. Project Editor: Barbara Booth
Consulting Editor: Rebecca Behan
Manager, English Book Editorial, Reader's Digest Canada: Pamela Johnson
Project Designer: Jennifer Tokarski
Managing Editor: Lorraine Burton
Senior Art Director: George McKeon
Editor-in-Chief, Books & Home Entertainment: Neil Wertheimer
Associate Publisher, Trade Publishing: Rosanne McManus
President and Publisher, Trade Publishing: Harold Clarke
President, Reader's Digest North America: Dan Lagani
Editor-in-Chief, Reader's Digest North America: Liz Vaccariello

Library of Congress Cataloging in Publication Data
I dare say : inside stories of the world's most powerful speeches / Ferdie Addis.
p. cm.

ISBN 978-1-60652-470-1 (alk. paper) -- ISBN 978-1-60652-471-8 (adobe) --
ISBN 978-1-60652-472-5 (epub)

1. Speeches, addresses, etc. 2. World history--Sources. 3. World politics--Sources. I. Addis, Ferdie, 1983-
PN6122.I22 2012
808.85--dc23

20110494

ISBN 978-1-60652-470-1

We are committed to both the quality of our products and the service we provide to our customers. We value your comments, so please feel free to contact us.

The Reader's Digest Association, Inc.
Adult Trade Publishing
44 South Broadway
White Plains, NY 10601

For more Reader's Digest products and information, visit our website:
www.rd.com (in the United States)
www.readersdigest.ca (in Canada)

Printed in the United States of America

1 3 5 7 9 10 8 6 4 2

But words are things, and a small drop of ink,
Falling like dew, upon a thought, produces
That which makes thousands, perhaps millions, think.

—George Gordon Byron

Contents

Introduction 9

The Classical Orations
8th–1st Centuries B.C. 13

Jesus of Nazareth
c. A.D. 26 The Sermon on the Mount 19

Pope Urban II
1096 The Council of Clermont 23

Oliver Cromwell
1653 Dismissing the Rump Parliament 27

Maximilien Robespierre
1794 The Political Philosophy of Terror 31

George Washington
1796 Farewell Address 35

Napoleon Bonaparte
1814 Farewell to the Old Guard 38

Sojourner Truth
1851 Aren't I a Woman? 42

Abraham Lincoln
1863 The Gettysburg Address 46

Chief Joseph
1877 I Will Fight No More Forever 50

Emmeline Pankhurst
1913 Freedom or Death 53

Mohandas Gandhi
1916 There Is No Salvation for India 57

Woodrow Wilson
1918 The Fourteen Points 61

Clarence Darrow and William Jennings Bryan
1925 Scopes Trial 65

Lou Gehrig
1939 Farewell to Baseball 69

Adolf Hitler
1939 First Soldier of the German Reich 72

Winston Churchill
1940 Three Wartime Speeches 77

Joseph Stalin
1941 Anniversary Celebration of the October Revolution 83

Franklin Delano Roosevelt
1941 A Date Which Will Live in Infamy 89

Jawaharlal Nehru
1947 A Tryst with Destiny 94

Mao Zedong
1949 The Chinese People Have Stood Up 98

Harold Macmillan
1960 Wind of Change 102

John F. Kennedy
1961 Inaugural Address 106

Martin Luther King, Jr.
1963 I Have a Dream 111

Barbara Jordan
1974 Today I Am an Inquisitor 118

Margaret Thatcher
1980 The Lady's Not for Turning 123

Ronald Reagan
1987 Tear Down This Wall! 127

Aung San Suu Kyi
1990 Freedom from Fear 132

Mary Fisher
1992 A Whisper of AIDS 136

Nelson Mandela
1994 Let Freedom Reign 139

Hillary Rodham Clinton
1995 Women's Rights Are Human Rights 144

Christopher Reeve
1996 American Family Values 148

Osama bin Laden
2001 Declaration of War on the United States 151

George W. Bush
2002 The Axis of Evil 155

Barack Obama
2008 Victory Speech 159

Sources 164

Acknowledgments 166

Index of Famous Lines 167

General Index 171

Introduction

A truly brilliant speech is an extraordinary thing. The great lines resonate with amazing power. Sometimes the secret lies in the rhythm of the words: "Fourscore and seven years ago our fathers brought forth on this continent . . ." Sometimes the art comes from a powerful metaphor or image: "The devil is not as terrible as he is painted." Sometimes a speech derives its impact from an ideal or a compelling vision: "I have a dream that my four little children will one day live in a nation where they will not be judged by the color of their skin, but by the content of their character."

These lines have lived on in our collective memories. It's impossible to think about the Battle of Britain, for example, without hearing Winston Churchill's gruff tones: "We shall fight on the beaches. We shall fight on the landing grounds . . ." No one could forget the words that rang forth from the first black U.S. president in November 2008, telling the world that "change has come to America."

But can a speech, however memorable, change history? Looking at the great sweep of civilization's story—the battles and revolutions, the marches and migrations, the economic upheavals—it would be easy to conclude that historical forces are much too vast and powerful to be affected by any single person, much less a single speech. In centuries past you might argue that old-fashioned chroniclers, with their focus on individuals, failed to see the forest for the trees.

But what if the opposite is true? To talk only in terms of nations and social forces, of entrenched cultural norms and demographic shifts, is to lose sight of the fact that history is made not by abstractions but by people—people with ambitions, feelings, desires, and, above all, ideas. When we ignore history's human dimension, we are failing to see the trees for the forest.

And although words can't fight battles or power factories, they certainly can drive people. There are times when people are in the grip of intense but inarticulate feelings. At those times the right speech can transform an incoherent surge of emotion into a burst of positive, directed activity. Barack Obama did this in his victory speech (pages 159-163). Hitler also used this power to achieve his own evil ends, channeling German resentment of economic woes into a murderous hatred of the Jews (pages 72-76).

At other times a speech can change the mood of a population—inspiring them with new courage or resolve. When Emmeline Pankhurst told women she was "a soldier temporarily absent from the fields of battle," she gave them new heart in the struggle for women's suffrage (page 53-56). When Franklin Roosevelt told his country of the Japanese attack on Pearl Harbor—a date that will live in infamy—he brought a newly resolute United States into World War II (pages 89-93).

And then there are times when a speech delivers an important message, such as when Jawaharlal Nehru announced the birth of India as a "tryst with destiny" (pages 94-97); Harold Macmillan marked the end of imperialism when he talked about the "wind of change" (pages 102-105); Malcolm X spoke of "the ballot or the bullet," warning the enemies of civil rights (pages 116-117).

This book is the story of these moments, when the words of a single man or woman changed the world. Some of the speeches will be familiar, others less so. They were made by priests, popes, peasants, slaves, soldiers, dictators, prime ministers, presidents, and Native American Indian chiefs. They were delivered from the distant corners of the globe. But they all have one thing in common: In one way or another, these speeches made history.

8th–1st Centuries B.C.

The Classical Orations

It was in ancient Greece that the art of rhetoric first began to flourish. The cramped city-states of the Greek world made perfect stages for orators to display their skills. And where power was relatively fragmented—as was the case in many cities—a persuasive speaker could wield considerable influence over small and easily swayed political assemblies.

In legal matters, too, the best speakers had a distinct advantage. In democratic Athens, cases were tried by large citizen juries—who appreciated fine words as much as solid argument. Indeed, one of literature's first heroes—Homer's Odysseus—was most admired not for his fighting skills but for his cunning way with words.

Like philosophy and science, rhetoric, too, was soon codified. Itinerant teachers called sophists gave lectures on the subject, and young Greek aristocrats flocked to their feet to learn the tricks of the trade. Aristotle, the tutor of Alexander the Great and also one of Greece's foremost intellectuals, laid out the rules of style and argument in the monumental work *The Art of Rhetoric.* Public speaking became the cornerstone of any proper education.

THE SPEECHES

Homer—*The Iliad*

Homer's *Iliad* is perhaps the first and greatest work in the whole of Western literature. It is also full of great speeches, of which the following is among the most famous. Agamemnon, high king of the Greeks, has insulted Achilles, the army's greatest fighter. In typically overblown style, Achilles offers his reply.

> *Wine-bibber . . . with the face of a dog and the heart of a hind, you never dare to go out with the host in fight, nor yet with our chosen men in ambuscade. You shun this as you do death itself.*
>
> *. . . Therefore I say, and swear it with a great oath . . . that hereafter they [the Greeks] shall look fondly for Achilles and shall not find him. In the day of your distress, when your men fall dying by the murderous hand of Hector, you shall not know how to help them, and shall rend your heart with rage for the hour when you offered insult to the best of the Achaeans.*

Pericles—Funeral Oration

Pericles was the greatest leader of ancient Athens and the man who most of all was responsible for establishing the city as the home of art, culture, and democracy. In this speech, which often has been held up as a masterpiece of the rhetorical arts, he is commemorating those who died in the first year of the Peloponnesian war against Sparta.

> *Such is the city for whose sake these men nobly fought and died; they could not bear the thought that she might be taken from them; and every one of us who survive should gladly toil on her behalf. . . .*
>
> *Such was the end of these men; they were worthy of Athens, and the living need not desire to have a more heroic spirit, although they may pray for a less fatal issue. The value of such a spirit is not to be expressed in words. . . .*
>
> *For the whole earth is the sepulchre of famous men; not only are they commemorated by columns and inscriptions in their own country, but in foreign lands there dwells also an unwritten memorial of them, graven not on stone but in the hearts of men. Make them your examples, and, esteeming courage to be freedom and freedom to be happiness, do not weigh too nicely the perils of war.*

Demosthenes—Third Philippic

Demosthenes was an Athenian statesman of the fourth century B.C. who devoted his life to the art of public speaking. It is said that when he was young, he used to train his voice by speaking with pebbles in his mouth or shouting over the roar of the waves.

His most famous speeches are the Philippics, so called because they dealt with Philip II of Macedon, a northern king who, Demosthenes was convinced, posed a mortal threat to Athenian freedom and democracy.

Despite Demosthenes' efforts, Athens fell to Philip's armies. But the Philippics lived on as rhetorical models for generations to come.

> *Many things could be named by the Olynthians today, which would have saved them from destruction if only they had then foreseen them. Many could be named by the Orites, many by the Phocians, many by every ruined city.*
>
> *But of what use to them is that? . . .*
>
> *So we too, Athenians, as long as we are safe, blessed with a very great city, ample advantages, and the fairest repute—what are we to do? Perhaps some of my hearers have long been eager to ask that question. . . . To begin with ourselves, we must make provision for our defense, I mean with war-galleys, funds, and men; for even if all other states succumb to slavery, we surely must fight the battle of liberty.*

Cicero—Thirteenth Philippic

Cicero was the finest orator ancient Rome ever produced. As a young man, his prowess in the courts was legendary—and feared. His speeches could ruin careers and demolish reputations.

His skill soon carried him to the forefront of Roman politics, just as the civil wars were tearing the Republic apart. His Philippics, named after Demosthenes' orations, were a set of fourteen speeches he made attacking Mark Antony, leader of one of the most powerful factions. At the time this speech (the thirteenth) was made, Antony was asking the Senate for peace. But Cicero was determined that there should be war.

You have repealed the acts of Marcus Antonius; you have taken down his laws; you have voted that they were carried by violence, and with a disregard of the auspices; you have called out the levies throughout all Italy; you have pronounced that colleague and ally of all wickedness a public enemy. What peace can there be with this man? Even if he were a foreign enemy, still, after such actions as have taken place, it would be scarcely possible, by any means whatever, to have peace. Though seas and mountains, and vast regions lay between you, still you would hate such a man without seeing him. But these men will stick to your eyes, and when they can, to your very throats; for what fences will be strong enough for us to restrain savage beasts?

THE CONSEQUENCES

The classical orators laid the foundation for centuries of argument, debate, reasoned thinking, and even sometimes outright manipulation. They were the teachers, celebrities, and history makers of their time. From their recorded speeches, generations of students learned the art of rhetoric. The methods of organizing and analyzing oral arguments that were developed in ancient Greece and Rome became building blocks in the Western educational canon, giving birth to the field of philosophy and influencing all aspects of daily life, from politics and the judicial system to religion and even poetry.

c. A.D. 26

The Sermon on the Mount

Jesus of Nazareth

(c. 5 B.C.–c. A.D. 30)

No one really knows when Jesus gave the Sermon on the Mount. In fact, concrete facts about Jesus's life are hard to come by. All we know for sure is that there was a Jewish preacher by that name who was crucified in Jerusalem sometime during the reign of the Roman emperor Tiberius. Beyond that, the details of his life are uncertain.

Nevertheless, he is credited with having made perhaps the most influential speech of all time—at least, if it was a speech, and if he made it. There are those who argue that what the Gospels present as a single sermon was in fact a poetic compilation of three years' worth of teachings.

But the facts of what happened are, perhaps, less important

than the story of what was believed to have happened, according to the Gospels written by Jesus's followers long after his death. These books, the central scriptures of Christianity, record a speech that, in the context of ancient religion, is truly revolutionary. Jesus took centuries of traditional Jewish law, handed down all the way from Moses, and stood them on their head.

THE SPEECH

The following is taken from the 1769 King James version of the Gospel of St. Matthew.

> *Blessed are the poor in spirit: for theirs is the kingdom of heaven.*
>
> *Blessed are they that mourn: for they shall be comforted.*
>
> *Blessed are the meek: for they shall inherit the earth.*
>
> *Blessed are they which do hunger and thirst after righteousness: for they shall be filled.*
>
> *Blessed are the merciful: for they shall obtain mercy.*
>
> *Blessed are the pure in heart: for they shall see God:*
>
> *Blessed are the peacemakers: for they shall be called the children of God.*
>
> *Blessed are they which are persecuted for righteousness' sake: for theirs is the kingdom of heaven.*
>
> *. . . Ye have heard that it was said by them of old time, Thou shalt not kill; and whosoever shall kill shall be in danger of the judgment:*
>
> *But I say unto you, that whosoever is angry with his brother without a cause shall be in danger of the judgment.*
>
> *. . .Ye have heard that it was said by them of old time, Thou shalt not commit adultery:*

But I say unto you, that whosoever looketh on a woman to lust after her hath committed adultery with her already in his heart.

. . . It hath been said, Whosoever shall put away his wife, let him give her a writing of divorcement:

But I say unto you, That whosoever shall put away his wife, saving for the cause of fornication, causeth her to commit adultery: and whosoever shall marry her that is divorced committeth adultery.

Again, ye have heard that it hath been said by them of old time, Thou shalt not forswear thyself, but shalt perform unto the Lord thine oaths:

But I say unto you, Swear not at all; neither by heaven; for it is God's throne;

Nor by the earth; for it is his footstool: neither by Jerusalem; for it is the city of the great King.

. . . Ye have heard that it hath been said, An eye for an eye, and a tooth for a tooth:

But I say unto you, That ye resist not evil: but whosoever shall smite thee on thy right cheek, turn to him the other also.

. . . After this manner therefore pray ye: Our Father which art in heaven, Hallowed be thy name.

Thy kingdom come. Thy will be done in earth, as it is in heaven.

Give us this day our daily bread.

And forgive us our debts, as we forgive our debtors.

And lead us not into temptation, but deliver us from evil: For thine is the kingdom, and the power, and the glory, for ever. Amen.

THE CONSEQUENCES

This speech sets out the foundation for a radical new system of religious belief. The old justice-based morality of "an eye for an eye" is replaced by a completely different set of rules, valuing meek self-effacement over righteous indignation.

Spread by the four evangelists, Mark, Matthew, Luke, and John, the message of the Gospels (literally "good news") proved powerful beyond imagining. Within 100 years of Jesus's death, the Roman emperor Nero was troubled by such large numbers of Christians that he took to setting them on fire to light his gardens.

Some 200 years after that, another emperor, Constantine the Great, saw which way the wind was blowing and made Christianity the official religion of the whole Roman Empire, from the forests of Germany to the Sahara Desert.

A thousand years later, as the Christian states of Europe started expanding their own empires, the message, if not the intent, of the Sermon was carried (sometimes at swordpoint) to the farthest corners of the globe. Today, in all its many forms, Christianity remains the most popular religion on the planet.

1096

The Council of Clermont

Pope Urban II

(c. 1035–1099)

By the end of the eleventh century, Western Europe was beginning to haul itself out of the long slump of the Dark Ages. The outlines of modern nations were emerging in the West; in the East a struggle between civilizations was reshaping the map. The Byzantine Empire, devastated by centuries of Islamic invasion, had been reduced to a tiny nub around its capital, Constantinople.

Eventually, in 1095, Byzantium's emperor, Alexius I Comnenus, swallowed his pride and sent word to Pope Urban II in Rome asking for help against the marauding infidels. Despite long-standing religious differences between East and West, Pope Urban was sympathetic to the plight of his fellow Christians. Apart from the obvious religious motives, a military mission to the East presented some rather more wordly benefits. Byzantium's lost empire was rich territory, a tempting bounty for land-starved western knights. And by uniting the West against a common enemy, Urban could hope to put an end to the constant petty feuding that still threatened to tear Europe apart.

So in 1096 the Pope held a gathering of clerics and kings at Clermont in France. There he made a speech that changed the course of the Middle Ages and left an indelible mark on Western culture.

THE SPEECH

The following is taken from Robert the Monk's account, written several decades after the speech.

> *Oh, race of Franks, race from across the mountains, race chosen and beloved by God . . . ! To you our discourse is addressed and for you our exhortation is intended. . . .*
>
> *From the confines of Jerusalem and the city of Constantinople a horrible tale has gone forth and very frequently has been brought to our ears, namely, that a race from the kingdom of the Persians, an accursed race, a race utterly alienated from God . . . has invaded the lands of those Christians and has depopulated them by the sword, pillage, and fire . . . They destroy the altars, after having defiled them with their uncleanness. They circumcise the Christians, and the blood of the circumcision they either spread upon the altars or pour into the vases of the baptismal font. When they wish to torture people by a base*

death, they perforate their navels, and dragging forth the extremity of the intestines, bind it to a stake; then with flogging they lead the victim around until, the viscera having gushed forth, the victim falls prostrate upon the ground. . . .

The kingdom of the Greeks is now dismembered by them and deprived of territory so vast in extent that it cannot be traversed in a march of two months. On whom therefore is the labor of avenging these wrongs and of recovering this territory incumbent, if not upon you? You, upon whom above other nations God has conferred remarkable glory in arms, great courage, bodily activity, and strength to humble the hairy scalp of those who resist you.

. . . Since this land you inhabit, shut in on all sides by the seas and surrounded by the mountain peaks, is too narrow for your large population; nor does it abound in wealth; and it furnishes scarcely food enough for its cultivators. Hence it is that you murder one another, that you wage war, and that frequently you perish by mutual wounds.

Let therefore hatred depart from among you, let your quarrels end, let wars cease, and let all dissensions and controversies slumber. Enter upon the road to the Holy Sepulchre [an ancient church marking the burial place of Christ]; wrest that land from the wicked race, and subject it to yourselves ... The land is fruitful above others, like another paradise of delights.

God has conferred upon you above all nations great glory in arms. Accordingly undertake this journey for the remission of your sins, with the assurance of the imperishable glory of the kingdom of heaven. . . .

THE CONSEQUENCES

Urban had aimed his speech at kings and princes, but so powerful was his message (and so compelling his promise of "remission of sins") that huge crowds of peasants trooped toward the Holy Land, armed with little more than pitchforks and blind faith. Of course, such armaments were little match for the disciplined Turkish archers who massacred them soon after they crossed into Asia.

But Europe's nobles had also obeyed the Pope's call. In 1099 a crusader army under the Count of Toulouse arrived at Jerusalem, which they then proceeded to sack and pillage in time-honored Western fashion.

Once the bloodshed was over, the crusaders discovered a culture that was in many ways more advanced than their own. Christian traders brought back silks and spices from the East. Western scholars translated Arabic texts, often themselves translations of forgotten works from ancient Greece.

Jerusalem stayed in crusader hands for less than 100 years, but it was from this cultural exchange that we get, for instance, the concepts of zero and algebra. It was not Pope Urban's intention, but it was after his words at Clermont that the West began to open its eyes to the wider world.

1653

Dismissing the Rump Parliament

Oliver Cromwell

(1599–1658)

Oliver Cromwell first came to prominence as a successful commander in the Parliamentarian army, fighting with the Roundheads against King Charles I's Cavaliers in the English Civil War. From 1642 to 1648, battles raged up and down Britain until at last the royalists were defeated.

In 1649, after long but unsuccessful negotiations, the stubborn king was executed by order of Parliament. Cromwell was by now the most powerful man in the country. His aim was then to establish a government of "saints"—pious men drawn from his own Congregationalist faith—but to do that constitutionally he needed the change to come from the so-called Rump Parliament, members who had stayed on after Charles's death. For years Cromwell waited for his glorious reformation. But as time went by, it became clear that the Rump Parliament's members were interested only in their own well-being.

Finally, in 1653, he could wait no longer. Accompanied by a group of soldiers, he appeared in the House of Commons and made the following blistering speech.

THE SPEECH

It is high time for me to put an end to your sitting in this place, which you have dishonored by your contempt of all virtue, and defiled by your practice of every vice.

Ye are a factious crew, and enemies to all good government. Ye are a pack of mercenary wretches, and would like Esau sell your country for a mess of pottage, and like Judas betray your God for a few pieces of money.

Is there a single virtue now remaining amongst you? Is there one vice you do not possess?

Ye have no more religion than my horse. Gold is your God. Which of you have not bartered your conscience for bribes? Is there a man amongst you that has the least care for the good of the Commonwealth?

Ye sordid prostitutes have you not defiled this sacred place, and turned the Lord's temple into a den of thieves, by your immoral principles and wicked practices?

Ye are grown intolerably odious to the whole nation. You were deputed here by the people to get grievances redressed, are yourselves become the greatest grievance.

Your country therefore calls upon me to cleanse this Augean stable, by putting a final period to your iniquitous proceedings in this House; and which by God's help, and the strength he has given me, I am now come to do.

I command ye therefore, upon the peril of your lives, to depart immediately out of this place.

Go, get you out! Make haste! Ye venal slaves be gone! So! Take away that shining bauble there, [indicating the ceremonial mace of office] and lock up the doors.

In the name of God, go!

THE CONSEQUENCES

Even by seventeenth-century standards this was an extraordinary piece of invective, delivered with the white-hot anger of an Old Testament prophet. This was Cromwell as God's messenger, sweeping away the corruption of the old parliamentary order.

After the dissolution of the Rump Parliament, the running of the state was taken up by the council of senior army officers, who at last established the long-hoped-for Parliament of Saints. But to Cromwell's dismay, this pious group of Protestant MPs proved no better than the last parliament. He had asked them to devise a program of reforms that would make England a truly godly country, but in December 1653, exhausted by petty squabbles, the Saints gave up and voted their own assembly out of existence.

Forced to admit that his experiment had failed, Cromwell took matters into his own hands, appointing himself lord protector in 1654. As head of state, he had taken the place of the king he had worked so hard to depose. Despite all his efforts, when Cromwell died in 1658, he left behind no political system that could survive him, and two years after his death the country reverted to the old monarchy under King Charles II. That monarchy has remained intact to this day.

OTHER NOTABLE LINES

Cromwell was not the first to chafe under monarchy's rule. Late in the fourteenth century, a traveling priest and full-time rabble-rouser named John Ball helped to organize the ultimately unsuccessful Peasants' Revolt. But before its (and his) demise, Ball delivered a speech that would go down in history for its argument against class-based society, beginning with the words, "When Adam delved and Eve span, who was then the gentleman?"

, he and nineteen others were sent
as, incidentally, the only execution
y more of his followers suffered the

o enforce his concept of virtue,
m became a threat to his own ideals.
beginning of the defeat of the Revo-
from the radicals to the conservatives,
re closed down, and freedom of wor-
February 1795.

1794

The Political Philosophy of Terror

Maximilien Robespierre

(1758–1794)

Robespierre was arguably the finest orator of the French Revolution. His background was in law, and as a young man he had campaigned to abolish the death penalty. However, his career took a change into politics, and in the months before the French Revolution, he became the leader of the radical Jacobin Club, which demanded exile or execution of the king and queen.

The mobs of Paris stormed the Tuileries Palace in 1792, and the Jacobins seized power. As leader of the Committee for Public Safety, Robespierre became the most powerful man in France. Faced with the threat of counter-revolution following the execution of Louis XIV, he masterminded a ruthless suppression of all opposition. Perhaps this corrupting influence of power changed his view on the sanctity of life. By July 1794, 2,400 people had been executed at the guillotine and countless more on the street in Robespierre's Reign of Terror.

In February 1794 Robespierre addressed the National Convention, defending his brutal methods for enforcing justice. The speech, though long (onlookers claimed he was on his feet for three hours), was eloquent, rousing, and chilling; the end absolutely justifies the means.

THE SPEECH

. . . But, to found and consolidate democracy, to achieve the peaceable reign of the constitutional laws, we must end the war of liberty against tyranny and pass safely across the storms of the revolution: such is the aim of the revolutionary system that you have enacted. Your conduct, then, ought also to be regulated by the stormy circumstances in which the republic is placed; and the plan of your administration must result from the spirit of the revolutionary government combined with the general principles of democracy.

Now, what is the fundamental principle of the democratic or popular government—that is, the essential spring which makes it move? It is virtue; I am speaking of the public virtue which effected so many prodigies in Greece and Rome and which ought to produce much more surprising ones in republican France; of that virtue which is nothing other than the love of country and of its laws.

outlaw. On July 28, 179
to the guillotine. This w
he ever witnessed. Eigh
same fate the next day.
In the struggle t
Robespierre's fanatici
His death marked the
lution. Power moved
the Jacobin Clubs w
ship was restored in

ar
is f
noth
there
princip
democra
It ha
governme
potism? Ye
heroes of lib
of tyranny ar
brutalized sub
ror the enemies
ers of the Repub
liberty's despotism
protect crime? And
the heads of the pro

THE C

This address to the conve
fect, of worse to come. T
the months that followed.
formed a conspiracy against
arrest was passed, Robespierr
vention, of which he was electe

1796

Farewell Address

George Washington

(1732–1799)

As a public servant, George Washington had commanded the Continental Army and defeated the British for colonial independence, which helped to assure the adoption of the Constitution. He was unanimously elected the first president of the newly formed United States of America. But in 1796 he was tired. Though he was urged to accept the nomination for a third term, Washington decided to retire.

During his final year of presidency, he worked with fellow statesmen James Madison and Alexander Hamilton to prepare his legacy—a farewell address to "friends and fellow citizens," delivered to the people via the newspaper rather than a public speech. Part love letter to his country, part admonition for the future, Washington focused on three threats he saw to the newly formed nation's well-being: geographic regionalism, the party system, and long-term foreign alliances.

THE SPEECH

I have already intimated to you the danger of parties in the State, with particular reference to the founding of them on geographical discriminations. Let me now take a more comprehensive view and warn you in the most solemn manner against the baneful effects of the spirit of party, generally.

This spirit, unfortunately, is inseparable from our nature, having its root in the strongest passions of the human mind. It exists under different shapes in all governments, more or less stifled, controlled, or repressed; but in those of the popular form it is seen in its greatest rankness and is truly their worst enemy. . . .

. . . It agitates the community with ill-founded jealousies and false alarms, kindles the animosity of one part against another, foments occasionally riot and insurrection. It opens the door to foreign influence and corruption, which find a facilitated access to the government itself through the channels of party passions. . . .

[Washington turns to foreign policy.]

. . . Just and amicable feelings towards all [nations] should be cultivated. The nation which indulges towards another an habitual hatred, or an habitual fondness, is in some degree a slave. . . .

So likewise, a passionate attachment of one nation for another produces a variety of evils. Sympathy for the favorite nation, facilitating the illusion of an imaginary common interest, in cases where no real common interest exists, and infusing into one the enmities of the other, betrays the former into a participation in the quarrels and wars of the latter. . . .

In offering to you, my countrymen, these counsels of an old and affectionate friend, I dare not hope they . . . may now and then recur to moderate the fury of party spirit, to warn against the mischiefs of foreign intrigue, [and] to guard against the impostures of pretended patriotism.

THE CONSEQUENCES

Washington's criticism of the two-party system would not gain traction, and his fears of regionalism were apt—the nation split into warring North and South factions some sixty years later during the Civil War. However, politicians did take Washington's exhortation on foreign policy to heart. The country would not form a long-standing major alliance until the close of World War II in 1941.

Today frequent references to the founding fathers and the birth of the nation are ever present in popular discourse, even when partisanship sometimes runs high in the U.S. political system.

1814

Farewell to the Old Guard

Napoleon Bonaparte

(1769–1821)

Napoleon Bonaparte was born into a family of modest rank. At military school they called him "the little corporal" because he was so short. And though he would someday become ruler of France, he was a native of Corsica and never lost his heavy Italian accent.

Nothing creates unlikely success stories like a revolution. In the years of chaos after the fall of the French monarchy in 1789, Napoleon rose swiftly through the ranks of the revolutionary army; in 1799 a bloodless coup made him first consul, and in 1804, at age 35, he rose to become emperor of France.

The country was surrounded by hostile powers, but

Napoleon was a superb general and smashed the ailing states of Austria and Prussia to create an empire that stretched from Portugal to the Baltic Sea. His "Grande Armée" was half a million strong.

Yet his power was not to last. In 1812 he took 400,000 men east toward Moscow. Six months later, devastated by the Russian winter, the frostbitten survivors of the Grande Armée came limping back.

By 1814 Napoleon was utterly defeated. The only soldiers that remained in his camp were the men of the Old Guard, an elite group of veteran troops utterly devoted to their emperor. Abandoned by his generals and encircled by enemy armies, Napoleon gathered the men and delivered the following speech.

THE SPEECH

Soldiers of my Old Guard:

I bid you farewell.

For twenty years I have constantly accompanied you on the road to honor and glory. In these latter times, as in the days of our prosperity, you have invariably been models of courage and fidelity.

With men such as you our cause could not be lost; but the war would have been interminable; it would have been civil war, and that would have entailed deeper misfortunes on France.

I have sacrificed all of my interests to those of the country.

I go, but you, my friends, will continue to serve France. Her happiness was my only thought. It will still be the object of my wishes.

Do not regret my fate; if I have consented to survive, it is to serve your glory. I intend to write the history of the great achievements we have performed together.

Adieu, my friends.

Would I could press you all to my heart.

THE CONSEQUENCES

With only 8,000 soldiers remaining against the combined armies of Europe, Napoleon was jumping before he could be pushed. But the Guardsmen appear to have bought his story. Some of them wept openly as Napoleon embraced their leader, General Petit, and cradled their eagle standard in his arms.

After this final farewell, Napoleon abdicated. He was exiled to Elba, in the Mediterranean, to rule as "emperor" over the island's population of peasants and goatherds.

But it soon became apparent that Napoleon intended to do more than just sit around writing history books. Less than a year later he escaped back to France, raised another army, and was marching north toward war.

Sent to meet him was the Duke of Wellington, England's finest general. On June 18, 1815, the armies clashed at the Battle of Waterloo. All day Napoleon threw his troops fruitlessly at the British line. Finally, in desperation, he ordered the Guard to advance.

But that day, for the first and last time, their strength failed him. Decimated by volley fire, facing British bayonets, and caught in the flank by a brilliantly timed charge of light infantry, the Guard broke and retreated—and as word of the Guard's retreat spread, the whole French army broke and ran. Napoleon was exiled again, this time to the island of Saint Helena, deep in the Atlantic, where he died in 1821.

OTHER NOTABLE LINES

The motto of the Republic of France—*Liberté, Égalité, Fraternité*—has its origins in the heady atmosphere of the eighteenth century, when the philosopher-tyrants of the French Revolution were building the principles for a new kind of state. It was one of a series of slogans. *Unité* once had a chance at joining the great triumvirate. So did *Raison* and *Sûreté.*

But over the course of the 1790s, it was the familiar three that became preeminent. What's less well known is that in its earliest incarnations the motto had a fourth, more bloodthirsty, part. As it appears on the oldest revolutionary placards, it reads: *Liberté, Égalité, Fraternité, ou la Mort*—Liberty, Equality, Fraternity, or Death!

1851

Aren't I a Woman?

Sojourner Truth

(c. 1799–1883)

Sojourner Truth was born into slavery in New York State around the turn of the nineteenth century. Known simply as Isabella, she served many owners before she was freed in 1827.

Along with her newfound freedom, Isabella found God, changed her name, and became a member of a succession of Methodist churches and unconventional religious movements, one of which preached that 1843 would mark the end of the world.

But as 1844 approached and the apocalypse failed to materialize, Sojourner Truth began to concern herself with more worldly problems, especially emancipation and women's rights. After a few small-town appearances, she addressed a convention of feminists in Akron, Ohio. With this speech she would step onto history's grand stage.

The audience had been browbeaten by a string of male preachers using selective quotations from the Bible to put rebellious women in their place. Then, amid gasps of racist outrage, the tall figure of Sojourner Truth slowly approached the speaker's platform.

Records of what she said are inconsistent, but the best-known account was written twelve years later by the feminist Frances Gage, who had presided at the meeting. It was her recollection of the speech that made Sojourner Truth a legend.

THE SPEECH

Well, children, where there is so much racket there must be something out of kilter. I think that 'twixt the Negroes of the South and the women at the North, all talking about rights, the white men will be in a fix pretty soon.

But what's all this here talking about? That man over there says that women need to be helped into carriages, and lifted over ditches, and to have the best place everywhere. Nobody ever helps me into carriages, or over mud-puddles, or gives me any best place. And aren't I a woman? Look at me! Look at my arm. I have plowed and planted and gathered into barns, and no man could head me. And aren't I a woman? I could work as much and eat as much as a man—when I could get it—and bear the lash as well. And aren't I a woman? I have borne thirteen children, and seen them most all sold off into slavery, and when I cried out with a mother's grief, none but Jesus heard me! And aren't I a woman?

Then they talk about this thing in the head; what's this they call it? ["Intellect," whispered someone near.]

That's it, honey. What's that got to do with women's rights or Negroes' rights? If my cup won't hold but a pint and yours holds a quart, wouldn't you be mean not to let me have my little half-measure full?

Then that little man in black there, he says women can't have as much rights as men, 'cause Christ wasn't a woman. Where did your Christ come from? Where did your Christ come from? Where did your Christ come from? From God and a woman! Man had nothing to do with Him.

If the first woman God ever made was strong enough to turn the world upside down all alone, these together ought to be able to turn it back and get it right side up again. And now they is asking to do it, the men better let them.

Obliged to you for hearing on me, and now old Sojourner hasn't got nothing more to say.

THE CONSEQUENCES

According to Gage, Truth left her audience with "streaming eyes, and hearts beating with gratitude." But Gage's account of the speech is untrustworthy. She gave Truth a cod southern dialect, although the speaker was from the North. She invented thirteen children for her, when she only had five. The most accurate reporting by Gage may be of Truth's physical presence. In her telling of the story, Gage admired Truth's "tremendous muscular power," a description seemingly corroborated by Harriet Beecher Stowe. The celebrated author of the novel *Uncle Tom's Cabin* was another of Truth's admirers, and although they met

1794

The Political Philosophy of Terror

Maximilien Robespierre

(1758–1794)

Robespierre was arguably the finest orator of the French Revolution. His background was in law, and as a young man he had campaigned to abolish the death penalty. However, his career took a change into politics, and in the months before the French Revolution, he became the leader of the radical Jacobin Club, which demanded exile or execution of the king and queen.

The mobs of Paris stormed the Tuileries Palace in 1792, and the Jacobins seized power. As leader of the Committee for Public Safety, Robespierre became the most powerful man in France. Faced with the threat of counter-revolution following the execution of Louis XIV, he masterminded a ruthless suppression of all opposition. Perhaps this corrupting influence of power changed his view on the sanctity of life. By July 1794, 2,400 people had been executed at the guillotine and countless more on the street in Robespierre's Reign of Terror.

In February 1794 Robespierre addressed the National Convention, defending his brutal methods for enforcing justice. The speech, though long (onlookers claimed he was on his feet for three hours), was eloquent, rousing, and chilling; the end absolutely justifies the means.

THE SPEECH

. . . But, to found and consolidate democracy, to achieve the peaceable reign of the constitutional laws, we must end the war of liberty against tyranny and pass safely across the storms of the revolution: such is the aim of the revolutionary system that you have enacted. Your conduct, then, ought also to be regulated by the stormy circumstances in which the republic is placed; and the plan of your administration must result from the spirit of the revolutionary government combined with the general principles of democracy.

Now, what is the fundamental principle of the democratic or popular government—that is, the essential spring which makes it move? It is virtue; I am speaking of the public virtue which effected so many prodigies in Greece and Rome and which ought to produce much more surprising ones in republican France; of that virtue which is nothing other than the love of country and of its laws.

But as the essence of the republic or of democracy is equality, it follows that the love of country necessarily includes the love of equality. . . .

If the spring of popular government in time of peace is virtue, the springs of popular government in revolution are at once virtue and terror: virtue, without which terror is fatal; terror, without which virtue is powerless. Terror is nothing other than justice, prompt, severe, inflexible; it is therefore an emanation of virtue; it is not so much a special principle as it is a consequence of the general principle of democracy applied to our country's most urgent needs.

It has been said that terror is the principle of despotic government. Does your government therefore resemble despotism? Yes, as the sword that gleams in the hands of the heroes of liberty resembles that with which the henchmen of tyranny are armed. Let the despot govern by terror his brutalized subjects; he is right, as a despot. Subdue by terror the enemies of liberty, and you will be right, as founders of the Republic. The government of the revolution is liberty's despotism against tyranny. Is force made only to protect crime? And is the thunderbolt not destined to strike the heads of the proud?

THE CONSEQUENCES

This address to the convention served as a warning, in effect, of worse to come. The Terror reached its apogee in the months that followed. Robespierre's political enemies formed a conspiracy against him. When a decree for his arrest was passed, Robespierre fled and the National Convention, of which he was elected president, declared him an outlaw. On July 28, 1794, he and nineteen others were sent to the guillotine. This was, incidentally, the only execution he ever witnessed. Eighty more of his followers suffered the same fate the next day.

In the struggle to enforce his concept of virtue, Robespierre's fanaticism became a threat to his own ideals. His death marked the beginning of the defeat of the Revolution. Power moved from the radicals to the conservatives, the Jacobin Clubs were closed down, and freedom of worship was restored in February 1795.

only once, Beecher commended her "wonderful physical vigor." Regardless of the accurateness of Gage's account, her record of the speech contributed to Truth's profile as an African-American feminist and abolitionist.

Sojourner Truth had become a myth, her true character buried beneath the stereotypes of her admirers. But although the myth was false, its impact was nonetheless deeply important. Her speech in Akron united the issues of slavery and women's rights and opened the western regions of the United States to her message. In 1863 Abraham Lincoln signed the Emancipation Proclamation. Slavery in the United States was finally over. Until her death, in 1883, Truth traveled throughout the country lecturing on suffrage and temperance, arguing for free land for former slaves and protesting segregation.

1863

The Gettysburg Address

Abraham Lincoln

(1809–1865)

Abraham Lincoln, sixteenth president of the United States, came from humble stock. He grew up in a crude three-sided shack in Pigeon Creek, Indiana, and served as a store clerk and postmaster before finally finding his true calling in politics.

Lincoln arrived in Congress in 1847 to find a body politic that was tearing itself apart. The crucial question was slavery, to which Lincoln was naturally opposed. The keeping of slaves, he wrote, "deprives our republican example of its just influence in the world—enables the enemies of free institutions, with plausibility, to taunt us as hypocrites. . . . Our republican robe is soiled, and trailed in the dust."

In 1860 Lincoln was elected president, which further alienated politicians from the slave-owning South. That year, the southern states formally seceded from the Union, and in 1861 this new Confederacy took up arms against their northern neighbors.

The Civil War ebbed and flowed across the continent as huge armies ground each other down with the new and terrible weapons of the Industrial Age. One of the bloodiest encounters was at Gettysburg in July 1863, where a northern army halted a southern advance, costing thousands of soldiers their lives.

So it was amid a mood of doubt and despondency that Abraham Lincoln traveled to the battlefield to give a short speech commemorating the fallen.

THE SPEECH

Fourscore and seven years ago our fathers brought forth on this continent a new nation, conceived in liberty and dedicated to the proposition that all men are created equal.

Now we are engaged in a great civil war, testing whether that nation or any nation so conceived and so dedicated can long endure. We are met on a great battlefield of that war. We have come to dedicate a portion of that field as a final resting-place for those who here gave their lives that that nation might live. It is altogether fitting and proper that we should do this.

But, in a larger sense, we cannot dedicate, we cannot consecrate, we cannot hallow this ground. The brave men, living and dead, who struggled here have consecrated it far above our poor power to add or detract. The world will little note nor long remember what we say here, but it can never forget what they did here.

It is for us the living rather to be dedicated here to the unfinished work which they who fought here have thus far so nobly advanced. It is rather for us to be here dedicated to the great task remaining before us—that from these honored dead we take increased devotion to that cause for which they gave the last full measure of devotion—that we here highly resolve that these dead shall not have died in vain, that this nation under God shall have a new birth of freedom, and that government of the people, by the people, for the people shall not perish from the earth.

THE CONSEQUENCES

According to popular legend, Lincoln wrote this speech while on the train from Washington, D.C. He wasn't even the main speaker. The townsfolk of Gettysburg had already engaged Edward Everett, a celebrated orator, to deliver the main address—a two-hour eulogy that was, by all accounts, rated a great success.

Lincoln, it is recorded, thought his speech had been a failure, and he was not alone. A reporter from *The Times* remarked: "The ceremony was rendered ludicrous by some of the luckless sallies of that poor President Lincoln."

But Lincoln and the reporter were both wrong. The Gettysburg Address is a rhetorical masterpiece and is now one of the most quoted speeches in history, often considered alongside the Constitution as a defining document of the United States. To be so remembered is no more than Lincoln deserves.

He was determined to see the war through to victory, and at last victory did come, ensuring that government "of the people, by the people, for the people" would survive the stern moral test that slavery and civil war had presented. Without Lincoln, the United States would be a different and lesser place today.

Sadly, Lincoln was not allowed much time to enjoy his victory. On April 15, 1865, he was shot by Confederate sympathizer John Wilkes Booth and died shortly after.

Today many American students memorize Lincoln's famous words, few in number but great in power and influence. Lincoln's vision of an America governed by politicians "of the people" and based on the principle of equality for all has become a prophecy that men and women yearned to fulfill.

OTHER NOTABLE LINES

Lincoln's words at Gettysburg harkened back to the ideals of the nation's founding, specifically those outlined in the Declaration of Independence. No document in history has had such an impact on the modern world as the one that was signed by the Continental Congress of American States on July 4, 1776, as it declared independence from Britain.

It was Thomas Jefferson who was most responsible for crafting the words that would create America. They were read in towns and villages across the new nation, and their echoes can still be heard today, defining the nature of what is now the most powerful country on Earth.

One of the most famous sentences in the English language comes at the very beginning—a bold and truly revolutionary statement of values:

"We hold these truths to be self-evident, that all men are created equal, that they are endowed by their creator with certain unalienable rights, that among these are life, liberty, and the pursuit of happiness."

1877

I Will Fight No More Forever

Chief Joseph

(c. 1840–1904)

By the 1870s, America's Indian Wars were reaching their final act. In the South, Apache war bands were mounting a fitful resistance; on the Great Plains, the Sioux were holding out; but by and large the battle for the Wild West was over.

In Wallowa Valley, Oregon, the Nez Percé tribe had suffered years of abuse from white settlers encroaching on their land. Their leader, Chief Joseph, knowing the might of the U.S. Army, argued desperately for peace. But in 1877 a band of Indian warriors lost patience and killed some white settlers near the Salmon River.

U.S. retaliation was not long coming, but the Nez Percé, with astonishing bravery, defeated the first detachment sent against them. Slowed down by women, children, and the wounded, Joseph and his tribe began a fighting retreat toward the wilds of the Pacific Northwest.

Finally, after traveling 1,170 miles across difficult country, they were intercepted by U.S. cavalry at Bear Paw Mountain in Montana, just forty miles from the safety of the Canadian border.

Joseph's warriors were cold, weakened, and outnumbered. So instead of fighting, the great chief did something that perhaps was braver. Meeting with the American officers, he made the following speech.

THE SPEECH

Tell General Howard [the American commander] I know his heart. What he told me before, I have it in my heart. I am tired of fighting. Our chiefs are killed; Looking Glass is dead, Too-hul-hul-sote is dead. The old men are all dead. It is the young men who say yes or no. He who led on the young men is dead.

It is cold, and we have no blankets; the little children are freezing to death. My people, some of them, have run away to the hills, and have no blankets, no food. No one knows where they are—perhaps freezing to death. I want to have time to look for my children, and see how many of them I can find. Maybe I shall find them among the dead.

Hear me, my chiefs! I am tired; my heart is sick and sad. From where the sun now stands, I will fight no more forever.

THE CONSEQUENCES

Chief Joseph never returned to his ancestral home. For years the Nez Percé were shuttled across the continent from one reservation to another, while disease and despair corroded their old way of life. Joseph campaigned tirelessly to be allowed to return to the Wallowa Valley, but despite the widespread sympathy that he earned, his request was never granted. In 1904 he died, according to his doctor, of a "broken heart."

But Joseph's great speech of surrender had a life of its own. It is probably the most quoted speech of any recorded by a Native American Indian, and no wonder. It is sad, short, simple, but at the same time an extraordinarily poetic testament to the suffering of a people. His final words, "I will fight no more forever," echoed on in national consciousness, and Joseph himself became a powerful symbol of the Native American Indian tragedy.

Even the name, Joseph, tells a story of the cultural vandalism that his people had suffered. His Indian title, which those two alien syllables replaced, was Hin-mut-too-uah-lat-kekht—Thunder Rolling in the Mountains.

1913

Freedom or Death

Emmeline Pankhurst

(1858–1928)

Literate from an early age, Emmeline Pankhurst was bright, focused, and politically aware. Certainly she was aware enough to realize very young that her life was to be circumscribed by an entrenched injustice. As a woman in Victorian England, her alloted destiny was to become a decorous helpmeet for some unappreciative man.

Barely out of her teens, Pankhurst started campaigning for female suffrage, and in 1903 she founded the organization that would make her famous—the Women's Social and Political Union, or WSPU. At first these suffragettes campaigned peacefully, but in 1908, tired of not being heard in the masculine confines of Westminster, the WSPU began a more militant program.

That February, Pankhurst served a month in prison for leading a deputation to the House of Commons. In 1909, WSPU members began hunger strikes and were force-fed. By 1913 they had started smashing shop windows, vandalizing artworks, and setting fires. Pankhurst even helped explode a bomb outside the house of the Chancellor of the Exchequer, David Lloyd-George.

She was arrested and sentenced to three years but was temporarily released after a string of hunger strikes. She took advantage of this brief moment of freedom to travel to the United States, where she made the following speech.

THE SPEECH

. . . I am here as a soldier who has temporarily left the field of battle in order to explain . . . what civil war is like when civil war is waged by women . . . I am here as a person who, according to the law courts of my country . . . is of no value to the community at all; and I am adjudged because of my life to be a dangerous person, under sentence of penal servitude in a convict prison. . . .

. . . Your forefathers decided that they must have representation for taxation, many, many years ago. When they felt they couldn't wait any longer, . . . when every other means had failed, they began by the tea party at Boston, and they went on until they had won the independence of the United States of America.

[. . .]

When you have warfare things happen; people suffer; the noncombatants suffer as well as the combatants. And so it happens in civil war. When your forefathers threw the tea into Boston Harbor, a good many women had to go without their tea …

[. . .]

Now, I want to say to you who think women cannot succeed, we have brought the government of England to this position, that it has to face this alternative: either women are to be killed or women are to have the vote. I ask American men in this meeting, what would you say if in your state you were faced with that alternative, that you must either kill them or give them their citizenship? Well, there is only one answer to that alternative, there is only one way out—you must give those women the vote.

… That is the way in which we women of England are doing. Human life for us is sacred, but we say if any life is to be sacrificed it shall be ours; we won't do it ourselves, but we will put the enemy in the position where they will have to choose between giving us freedom or giving us death.

[. . .]

THE CONSEQUENCES

Emmeline's case was brilliantly calibrated to win over her American audience with her references to soldiers and civil war, and her paraphrasing of the American Revolutionary John Henry, who famously declared: "Give me liberty, or give me death!"

But Pankhurst's real genius was to realize that the key was to be heard at all. Although her methods might have been extreme, they worked, and the suffragette argument proved too powerful to be fought back for long. In

February 1918, Parliament announced that all women over thirty would henceforth have the vote. In 1928 a new bill was set to give that right to all women over 21. That year, a month before the bill was passed, Emmeline Pankhurst died, at the age of 69.

1916

There Is No Salvation for India

Mohandas Gandhi

(1869–1948)

Born in Queen Victoria's India, at the height of the British Raj, Mohandas Gandhi's early life exposed him to both sides of the British Empire. In London, where like many of his compatriots, he trained to be a lawyer, Gandhi saw the imperial capital in all its splendor. But soon after qualifying, he took a legal post in British-ruled South Africa, where he saw colonialism and racism at its worst.

For twenty years Gandhi was a tireless campaigner for South African civil rights. It was there that he developed his philosophy of *satyagraha,* a doctrine of nonviolent resistance that encouraged honesty, cooperation, and compassion and deplored more warlike methods of opposition.

Gandhi had a deep impact on South Africa, but when he returned to India in 1915, he was still a relative unknown. However, that would soon change. In 1916 he gave one of his first public speeches in India to an audience of students, aristocrats, and colonial grandees at the opening of a new university in Benares. It was this speech that put Gandhi firmly on the map.

THE SPEECH

I want to think audibly this evening. I do not want to make a speech and if you find me this evening speaking without reserve, pray, consider that you are only sharing the thoughts of a man who allows himself to think audibly, and if you think that I seem to transgress the limits that courtesy imposes upon me, pardon me for the liberty I may be taking. . . .

I have turned the searchlight all over, and as you have given me the privilege of speaking to you, I am laying my heart bare. Surely we must set these things right in our progress towards self-government. I now introduce you to another scene. His Highness the Maharaja who presided yesterday over our deliberations spoke about the poverty of India. Other speakers laid great stress upon it. But what did we witness in the great pandal [a temporary religious structure] in which the foundation ceremony was performed by the Viceroy? Certainly a most gorgeous show, an exhibition of jewelry, which made a splendid feast for the eyes of the greatest jeweler who chose to come from Paris. I compare with the richly bedecked noblemen the millions of the poor. And I feel like saying to these noblemen, "There is no salvation for India unless you strip yourselves of this jewelry and hold it in trust for your countrymen in India." I am sure it is not the desire of the king-emperor . . . that in order to show the truest loyalty . . . it is necessary for us to ransack our jewelry boxes and to appear bedecked from top to toe. I would undertake, at the peril of my life, to bring to you a message from King George himself that he expects nothing of the kind.

Sir, whenever I hear of a great palace rising in any great city of India, be it in British India or be it in India which is ruled by our great chiefs, I become jealous at once, and say, "Oh, it is the money that has come from the agriculturists." Over seventy-five percent of the population are agriculturists and Mr. Higginbotham told us last night in his own felicitous language, that they are the men who grow two blades of grass in the place of one. But there cannot be much spirit of self-government about us, if we take away or allow others to take away from them almost the whole of the results of their labor. Our salvation can only come through the farmer. Neither the lawyers, nor the doctors, nor the rich landlords are going to secure it.

THE CONSEQUENCES

When Gandhi gave this speech, Indian nationalism had been steadily gaining momentum. A generation of highly educated Indians were chafing under the iniquities of British rule. The Indian National Congress, formed in 1885, had been agitating for greater independence from Britain. There had been growing unrest, too. In 1912 the Viceroy, Lord Hardinge, had narrowly survived an assassination attempt.

Gandhi agreed that independence was desirable, but his approach to winning it was revolutionary. To achieve true independence, he argued, his country would have to prove itself worthy. Instead of turning his "spotlight" on the British overlords, Gandhi directed it toward India itself.

The glittering princes in the audience were not pleased by his remarks about wealth, extravagance, and the common man. Nor did the rest of his speech go much better. Long before he reached his conclusion, Gandhi was hastily hurried from the stage.

But his bold new path to independence did catch on. By the 1920s Gandhi had become a sort of living saint in India—a popular hero whose every move provoked passion from the people and fear in their colonial masters. In 1947, after decades of struggle, the British finally relinquished their grip. Gandhi, his mission accomplished, was assassinated the following year.

1918

The Fourteen Points

Woodrow Wilson

(1856–1924)

When war exploded across Europe in 1914, President Woodrow Wilson determined to stay neutral. But just one year after his election to the presidency of the United States, the four major European powers—the Austro-Hungarian, German, Ottoman, and Russian empires—had split into factions, the Allies versus the Central Powers.

Wilson attempted to mediate peace, but his efforts were rebuffed, and though he managed to keep the United States out of war for years, Germany's attacks on U.S. ships propelled the nation to war. His speech to Congress in January 1918, nine months after the country had formally entered the conflict, addressed the causes of World War I and his vision for peace in fourteen concise points, excerpted here. These basic principles would become the beginning of peace negotiations between European nations—and the basis for future American foreign policy.

THE SPEECH

We entered this war because violations of right had occurred which touched us to the quick and made the life of our own people impossible unless they were corrected and the world secure once for all against their recurrence. What we demand in this war, therefore, is nothing peculiar to ourselves. It is that the world be made fit and safe to live in; and particularly that it be made safe for every peace-loving nation which, like our own, wishes to live its own life, determine its own institutions, be assured of justice and fair dealing by the other peoples of the world as against force and selfish aggression. All the peoples of the world are in effect partners in this interest, and for our own part we see very clearly that unless justice be done to others it will not be done to us. The program of the world's peace, therefore, is our program; and that program, the only possible program, as we see it, is this:

I. Open covenants of peace, openly arrived at, after which there shall be no private international understandings of any kind . . .

II. Absolute freedom of navigation upon the seas, outside territorial waters, alike in peace and in war . . .

III. The removal, so far as possible, of all economic barriers and the establishment of an equality of trade conditions . . .

IV. Adequate guarantees given and taken that national armaments will be reduced to the lowest point consistent with domestic safety.

V. A free, open-minded, and absolutely impartial adjustment of all colonial claims . . .

VI. The evacuation of all Russian territory and such a settlement of all questions affecting Russia as will secure the best and freest cooperation of the other nations of the world . . .

VII. Belgium, the whole world will agree, must be evacuated and restored . . .

VIII. All French territory should be freed and the invaded portions restored . . .

IX. A readjustment of the frontiers of Italy should be effected along clearly recognizable lines of nationality.

X. The peoples of Austria-Hungary, whose place among the nations we wish to see safeguarded and assured, should be accorded the freest opportunity to autonomous development.

XI. Romania, Serbia, and Montenegro should be evacuated . . .

XII. The Turkish portion of the present Ottoman Empire should be assured a secure sovereignty . . .

XIII. An independent Polish state should be erected which should include the territories inhabited by indisputably Polish populations . . .

XIV. A general association of nations must be formed under specific covenants for the purpose of affording mutual guarantees of political independence and territorial integrity to great and small states alike. . . .

. . . The moral climax of this the culminating and final war for human liberty has come, and they [the people of the United States] are ready to put their own strength, their own highest purpose, their own integrity and devotion to the test.

THE CONSEQUENCES

Leaflets of the speech were dropped behind enemy lines and the message broadcast at home. Wilson's belief that "the world be made safe to live in" resonated with the American public and connected the idea of international security with a domestic agenda. He believed that a lasting peace could be forged only via an ethical and moral code rather than self-interest, and he advocated free trade, self-determination for those under colonial rule, and a world organization dedicated to peace—the League of Nations.

Ultimately, the Treaty of Versailles that ended the war adopted few of Wilson's points, and the U.S. Senate declined to enter America into the League of Nations. However, Wilson's ideals formed the basis for continuing U.S. foreign policy and the future United Nations.

1925

Scopes Trial

Clarence Darrow (1857–1938)
William Jennings Bryan (1860–1925)

ntific advancements of earlier centuries gained
n the United States, there was one idea that split
dicial opinion: the origin of the species. States
ohibiting the teaching of evolution in public
ough it often was included in textbooks. A
n Dayton, Tennessee, decided to challenge
ing together two of the most famous
awyer Clarence Darrow, who would de-
ight to teach evolution, and statesman
an, who would assist the prosecution.
in carnival fashion, and thousands of
ts converged on the small southern
peech of the trial was not a speech,
een these two men.

THE SPEECH

Darrow: *. . . You have given considerable study to the Bible, haven't you, Mr. Bryan?*

Bryan: *Yes, sir, I have tried to. . . .*

Darrow: *Do you claim that everything in the Bible should be literally interpreted?*

Bryan: *I believe everything in the Bible should be accepted as it is given there. . . .*

[Darrow and Bryan sparred on many points, including biblical stories. Bryan testified that he believed some recorded events to be miracles and could be interpreted in more than one way. Darrow eventually brought the line of questioning to creation.]

Darrow: *Then when the Bible said, for instance, "And God called the firmament heaven, and the evening and the morning were the second day," that does not necessarily mean twenty-four hours? . . .*

Bryan: *I do not think they were twenty-four-hour days. . . . I think it would be just as easy for the kind of God we believe in to make the Earth in six days as in six years or in six million years or in six hundred millio years. I do not think it important whether we believe o or the other. . . . My impression is that they were perio but I would not attempt to argue as against anybody w wanted to believe in literal days.*

Darrow: *Have you any idea of the length of the peri*

Bryan: *No, I don't.*

Darrow: *Do you think the sun was made o fourth day?*

1925

Scopes Trial

Clarence Darrow (1857–1938) **William Jennings Bryan** (1860–1925)

As the scientific advancements of earlier centuries gained acceptance in the United States, there was one idea that split public and judicial opinion: the origin of the species. States passed laws prohibiting the teaching of evolution in public schools, even though it often was included in textbooks. A group of people in Dayton, Tennessee, decided to challenge these laws, bringing together two of the most famous orators of the day: lawyer Clarence Darrow, who would defend John Scopes's right to teach evolution, and statesman William Jennings Bryan, who would assist the prosecution.

The trial unfolded in carnival fashion, and thousands of spectators and journalists converged on the small southern town. The most famous speech of the trial was not a speech, per se, but a dialogue between these two men.

THE SPEECH

Darrow: . . . You have given considerable study to the Bible, haven't you, Mr. Bryan?

Bryan: Yes, sir, I have tried to. . . .

Darrow: Do you claim that everything in the Bible should be literally interpreted?

Bryan: I believe everything in the Bible should be accepted as it is given there. . . .

[Darrow and Bryan sparred on many points, including biblical stories. Bryan testified that he believed some recorded events to be miracles and could be interpreted in more than one way. Darrow eventually brought the line of questioning to creation.]

Darrow: Then when the Bible said, for instance, "And God called the firmament heaven, and the evening and the morning were the second day," that does not necessarily mean twenty-four hours? . . .

Bryan: I do not think they were twenty-four-hour days. . . . I think it would be just as easy for the kind of God we believe in to make the Earth in six days as in six years or in six million years or in six hundred million years. I do not think it important whether we believe one or the other. . . . My impression is that they were periods, but I would not attempt to argue as against anybody who wanted to believe in literal days.

Darrow: Have you any idea of the length of the periods?

Bryan: No, I don't.

Darrow: Do you think the sun was made on the fourth day?

Bryan: *Yes.*

Darrow: *And they had evening and morning without the sun?*

Bryan: *I am simply saying it was a period. . . .*

Darrow: *And they had the evening and the morning before that time for three days or three periods. All right, that settles it. Now, if you call those periods, they might have been a very long time.*

Bryan: *They might have been.*

Darrow: *The creation might have been going on for a very long time?*

Bryan: *It might have continued for millions of years. . . . Your Honor, I think I can shorten this testimony. The only purpose Mr. Darrow has is to slur at the Bible, but I will answer his question. I will answer it all at once, and I have no objection in the world. I want the world to know that this man, who does not believe in a God, is trying to use a court in Tennessee . . . to slur at it, and, while it will require time, I am willing to take it.*

THE CONSEQUENCES

The trial had been moved to the lawn outside the courthouse because of the crush of spectators. Throughout the interrogation, held over the objections of council and amid laughter and applause from the crowd, Bryan remained resolute in continuing the questioning, though Darrow's inquiries frequently elicited a response of "I don't know."

The men argued over the larger issue—whether religion should have a place at the state-sponsored education table. As Darrow put it in his opening remarks, "I am going to argue it [this case] . . . as if it was a death struggle between two civilizations"—the Victorian-era past and the modern, scientific world.

The judge cut off the questioning and ruled that the debate was not admissible. The defense lost its case in the courts but won in the court of public opinion. Yet even today the place of religion in public schools remains a heated issue.

1939

Farewell to Baseball

Lou Gehrig

(1903–1941)

The early twentieth century signaled great change in America, and it was at this time that the sport of baseball moved from farming towns to urban environs, reflected in the melting pot of the great city stadiums such as Wrigley Field in Chicago and Yankee Stadium in New York. Baseball was for everyone, and it was king.

Into this environment stepped Lou Gehrig, the son of hardworking German immigrants to New York City. He signed with the Yankees at age 20 while still an engineering student at Columbia University and would proudly wear the pinstriped uniform for the next 16 years, playing 2,130 consecutive games and setting record after record, with Babe Ruth and Joe DiMaggio at his side.

Lou Gehrig had achieved the status of American hero

when he said good-bye to baseball on July 4, 1939—Independence Day. Just two months after he left the game, 60,000 people had gathered to watch the New York Yankees versus the Washington Senators and to honor the man who now stood before them, head bowed, to announce his formal retirement.

THE SPEECH

Fans, for the past two weeks you have been reading about the bad break I got. Yet today I consider myself the luckiest man on the face of this earth. I have been in ballparks for seventeen years and have never received anything but kindness and encouragement from you fans.

Look at these grand men. Which of you wouldn't consider it the highlight of his career just to associate with them for even one day? . . .

When the New York Giants, a team you would give your right arm to beat, and vice versa, sends you a gift—that's something. When everybody down to the groundskeepers and those boys in white coats remember you with trophies—that's something. When you have a wonderful mother-in-law who takes sides with you in squabbles with her own daughter—that's something. When you have a father and a mother who work all their lives so you can have an education and build your body—it's a blessing. When you have a wife who has been a tower of strength and shown more courage than you dreamed existed—that's the finest I know.

So I close in saying that I might have been given a bad break, but I've got an awful lot to live for.

THE CONSEQUENCES

Gehrig's "bad break" was worse than most people might have imagined. The game's Iron Horse—so nicknamed for his endurance—had been diagnosed with a degenerative neurological disease called amyotrophic lateral sclerosis (ALS). On the day of his farewell, he struggled to walk to the microphone and could not hold the trophies and gifts presented to him. Yet his humble words of gratitude did not reflect on the hard times ahead or on the past glories of his career. Instead, he focused on others—his family, colleagues, and loyal fans.

Gehrig died on June 2, 1941, and the nation mourned. His widow received 1,500 messages of condolence from around the country, and even President Franklin Delano Roosevelt sent her flowers of remembrance. Today the disease that took his life bears his name, and researchers continue seeking a cause and cure for Lou Gehrig's Disease.

1939

First Soldier of the German Reich

Adolf Hitler

(1889–1945)

No politician in history has used the power of rhetoric to more evil effect than Adolf Hitler. At mass rallies he would whip his audiences into a frenzy—listeners wept and laughed, hanging on every word, shouting their support in great choruses of *sieg heil.*

Except for this malign talent, Hitler had little to arm him in his struggle to conquer Germany's soul. He had been an unexceptional student and had fought as a lowly lance corporal in the World War I.

But as Hitler turned to extreme nationalist politics after the war, his ability to play on grievances and stir up anger proved to be an unbeatable weapon. By 1921 he had risen to become leader of what would become the Nazi party, and his fiery speeches soon attracted more followers to the growing movement.

Despite a spell in prison after the failed Munich Putsch and a subsequent ban on public speaking, Hitler's momentum was unstoppable. In 1933, with his popularity soaring, he was appointed chancellor of the German Republic. Soon after, through a combination of political bullying and paramilitary violence, he abolished the republic altogether, replacing it with a new "Third Reich."

Six years later, on September 1, 1939, with this speech, Hitler announced to his ministers that Germany was going to war with Poland.

THE SPEECH

For months we have been suffering under the torture of a problem which the Versailles Diktat created [the occupation by Poland of the Danzig Corridor after the end of World War I]—a problem which has deteriorated until it becomes intolerable for us . . .

As always, I attempted to bring about, by the peaceful method of making proposals for revision, an alteration of this intolerable position . . . On my own initiative I have, not once but several times, made proposals for the revision of intolerable conditions. All these proposals, as you know, have been rejected . . . It was all in vain. . . .

. . . I am wrongly judged if my love of peace and my patience are mistaken for weakness or even cowardice. I, therefore, decided last night and informed the British government that in these circumstances I can no longer find

any willingness on the part of the Polish government to conduct serious negotiations with us. . . .

I am asking of no German man more than I myself was ready throughout four years at any time to do. There will be no hardships for Germans to which I myself will not submit. My whole life henceforth belongs more than ever to my people. I am from now on just first soldier of the German Reich. I have once more put on that coat that was the most sacred and dear to me. I will not take it off again until victory is secured, or I will not survive the outcome. . . .

As a National Socialist and as a German soldier I enter upon this struggle with a stout heart. My whole life has been nothing but one long struggle for my people, for its restoration, and for Germany. There was only one watchword for that struggle: faith in this people. One word I have never learned: that is, surrender.

. . . I would, therefore, like to assure all the world that a November 1918 [Germany's surrender in World War I] will never be repeated in German history.

[. . .]

And I would like to close with the declaration that I once made when I began the struggle for power in the Reich. I then said: "If our will is so strong that no hardship and suffering can subdue it, then our will and our German might shall prevail."

THE CONSEQUENCES

Looked at in hindsight, this speech is an astonishing catalog of lies. Every undertaking, every solemn declaration, was broken within a few short years. All Hitler's fulminations about imagined grievances were nothing more than a shameless pretext. Germany was being launched into total war.

France and Britain had guaranteed Polish independence. When the Germans attacked, the two Western powers had no choice but to support their ally. In 1941 Germany attacked Russia despite a secret Nazi–Soviet pact signed in August 1939, under which the Soviet Union invaded eastern Poland on September 17. Later in 1941 the United States joined the fight, following the Japanese surprise attack at Pearl Harbor.

Of all the lies in Hitler's speech, the greatest was that Germany's war of aggression would be victorious. By 1945 the vaunted Nazi army had been decimated. Across the world, 60 to 80 million people had been killed. Some 6 million Jews had perished in the genocide of the Holocaust, along with a similar number made up of Slavs, homosexuals, communists, Gypsies, and others. As spring arrived in Europe, Soviet troops advanced into the streets of a shattered Berlin.

Far below the burning city, Hitler, knowing he was finished, committed suicide. In that one act, at least, he kept his word.

OTHER NOTABLE LINES

British prime minster Neville Chamberlain was not a bad leader. He has, however, had the misfortune to be remembered for his one catastrophic error of judgment.

It was 1938, and Chamberlain had just returned from Germany where he had been meeting Adolf Hitler. At that meeting, Hitler had accepted a deal that gave him control of the German-populated Czech region of the Sudetenland.

Deprived of this mountainous frontier, Czechoslovakia was defenseless before the German war machine, but Hitler had promised that after the Sudetenland, he had no more territorial ambitions in Europe. So when Chamberlain landed, he brandished his newly signed agreement at the crowds and spoke the oft-misquoted words: "I believe it is peace for our time."

1940

Three Wartime Speeches

Winston Churchill

(1874–1965)

Winston Churchill did not have an auspicious childhood. "If you cannot prevent yourself," his frustrated father once wrote, "from leading the idle useless unprofitable life you have had during your schooldays ... you will become a mere social wastrel." And as a young man, despite his clear potential, he made as many enemies as friends.

When, after a successful career as a soldier and war correspondent, he decided to enter politics, his headstrong ways and willingness to speak his mind always held him back from the highest office. Throughout the 1930s, for example, he was a thorn in the side of the government, constantly warning unwilling listeners of the deadly threat posed by the newly powerful Nazi regime.

But when Hitler invaded Czechoslovakia and then Poland in 1939, Churchill was proved suddenly and terrifyingly right. In May 1940 he became prime minister.

THE SPEECHES

May 13, 1940—Blood, Toil, Tears and Sweat

This was Churchill's first speech to the House of Commons as prime minister. The previous night, German troops had crossed into Belgium, the Netherlands, and Luxembourg. The Battle of France had begun.

> *I would say to the House, as I said to those who have joined this government: "I have nothing to offer but blood, toil, tears, and sweat." We have before us an ordeal of the most grievous kind. We have before us many, many long months of struggle and of suffering. You ask, what is our policy? I can say: It is to wage war, by sea, land and air, with all our might and with all the strength that God can give us; to wage war against a monstrous tyranny, never surpassed in the dark, lamentable catalog of human crime. That is our policy. You ask, what is our aim? I can answer in one word: It is victory, victory at all costs, victory in spite of all terror, victory, however long and hard the road may be; for without victory, there is no survival. Let that be realized; no survival for the British Empire, no survival for all that the British Empire has stood for, no survival for the urge and impulse of the ages, that mankind will move forward towards its goal. But I take up my task with*

buoyancy and hope. I feel sure that our cause will not be suffered to fail among men. At this time I feel entitled to claim the aid of all, and I say, "come then, let us go forward together with our united strength."

June 4, 1940—We Shall Fight on the Beaches

Churchill delivered this speech not long after the successful evacuation of the British Expeditionary Force from Dunkirk. After a stirring account of the operation, and the heroism of those who made it possible, Churchill continues:

Nevertheless, our thankfulness at the escape of our army and so many men, whose loved ones have passed through an agonizing week, must not blind us to the fact that what has happened in France and Belgium is a colossal military disaster. The French army has been weakened, the Belgian army has been lost, a large part of those fortified lines upon which so much faith had been reposed is gone, many valuable mining districts and factories have passed into the enemy's possession, the whole of the Channel ports are in his hands, with all the tragic consequences that follow from that, and we must expect another blow to be struck almost immediately at us or at France. . . .

. . . Even though large tracts of Europe and many old and famous states have fallen or may fall into the grip of the Gestapo and all the odious apparatus of Nazi rule, we shall not flag or fail. We shall go on to the end, we shall fight in France, we shall fight on the seas and oceans, we shall fight with growing confidence and growing strength in the air, we shall defend our island, whatever the cost may be, we shall fight on the beaches, we shall fight on

the landing grounds, we shall fight in the fields and in the streets, we shall fight in the hills; we shall never surrender, and even if, which I do not for a moment believe, this island or a large part of it were subjugated and starving, then our empire beyond the seas, armed and guarded by the British fleet, would carry on the struggle, until, in God's good time, the New World, with all its power and might, steps forth to the rescue and the liberation of the old.

June 18, 1940—Their Finest Hour

By the time Churchill made this speech, France was utterly defeated. Churchill spent much of the time talking up the strength of British defenses against invasion, but he left no doubt as to what was at stake:

What General Weygand [the French commander in chief] called the Battle of France is over. I expect that the Battle of Britain is about to begin. Upon this battle depends the survival of Christian civilization. Upon it depends our own British life, and the long continuity of our institutions and our empire.

The whole fury and might of the enemy must very soon be turned on us. Hitler knows that he will have to break us in this island or lose the war. If we can stand up to him, all Europe may be free and the life of the world may move forward into broad, sunlit uplands. But if we fail, then the whole world, including the United States, including all that we have known and cared for, will sink into the abyss of a new Dark Age made more sinister, and perhaps more protracted, by the lights of perverted science.

Let us therefore brace ourselves to our duties, and so bear ourselves that, if the British Empire and its Commonwealth last for a thousand years, men will still say, "This was their finest hour."

THE CONSEQUENCES

Years earlier, during World War I, Churchill had written to his wife: "Everything tends towards catastrophe and collapse. I am interested, geared up and happy. Is it not horrible to be built like that?"

Now, in a position of far greater responsibility and with a far worse disaster looming, he was inspired to new heights and his speeches, broadcast on the BBC, inspired his countrymen.

Britain had every reason to fear Hitler. And the example of France—which surrendered despite having a largely intact navy and huge numbers of men still under arms—had shown the importance of national morale. Within a month of Churchill's "Finest Hour" speech, the first German bombers had struck at British cities. That August, as Fighter Command struggled to hold off the Luftwaffe, Churchill immortalized the RAF's pilots: "Never in the field of human conflict was so much owed by so many to so few."

But the country held its nerve. The Battle of Britain was won by the year's end, and slowly the tide began to turn. In November 1942 Churchill was able to comment on the British victory at El Alamein in North Africa: "This is not the end. It is not even the beginning of the end. But it is, perhaps, the end of the beginning."

OTHER NOTABLE LINES

Guiseppe Garibaldi grew up in a divided Italy. A patchwork of small Italian states feuded with each other, or labored under the rule of foreign masters.

So in 1848 he embarked on a mission to wipe away the fractious old order and create a new Italian republic in its stead. His initial efforts did not go to plan. In 1849 he found himself in Rome, wounded and defeated, and facing the prospect of surrender to a besieging French army. Defiant, he addressed a crowd in St Peter's Square:

"Soldiers, I am going out from Rome. Let those who wish to continue the war against the stranger, come with me. I offer neither pay, nor quarters, nor provisions. I offer hunger, thirst, forced marches, battles and death. Let him who loves his country follow me."

It took over a decade, but Garibaldi's dream of a unified nation was finally realized, and he is remembered as the father of modern Italy. Years later Winston Churchill's "Blood, Toil, Tears and Sweat" speech drew inspiration from Garibaldi's famous words.

1941

Anniversary Celebration of the October Revolution

Joseph Stalin

(1878–1953)

Born Iosif Vissarionovich Dzhugashvili, Joseph Stalin rose from the poverty endured by most peasants in late-nineteenth-century Russia to study at the Tiflis Theological Seminary.

Stalin never graduated; instead he joined a secret organization, mixing with social revolutionaries and reading Marxist literature. In 1901 he joined the Social Democratic Labor Party and two years later the Bolsheviks. He was repeatedly arrested for his political actions and at one point exiled to Siberia.

Stalin assisted Vladimir Lenin in organizing a Bolshevik uprising and was elected general secretary of the newly named Communist party in 1922, allowing him to build up a base of support.

After Lenin's death in 1924, Stalin won the power struggle to succeed him. As the supreme ruler of the Soviet Union, Stalin enforced rapid industrialization, increasing Soviet productivity and economic growth. However, his regime of terror, during which he staged purges that rid the party of "enemies of the people," resulted in the execution of thousands and the suffering of millions more who were forced into exile.

These purges severely depleted the Red Army and, when Germany invaded Russia on June 22, 1941, Stalin was caught off guard. His ruthlessness won through, and in a series of speeches, he rallied the population, calling for a scorched-earth policy that would deny the Germans any supplies. In this speech, given in Red Square on November 7, 1941, the anniversary of the October Revolution, Stalin shows that he is prepared to fight the Germans and that neither he, nor the army, would give in.

THE SPEECH

Comrades, today we must celebrate the 24th anniversary of the October Revolution in difficult conditions. The German brigands' treacherous attack and the war that they forced upon us have created a threat to our country. We have temporarily lost a number of regions, and the enemy is before the gates of Leningrad and Moscow.

The enemy calculated that our army would be dispersed at the very first blow and our country forced to its knees. But the enemy wholly miscalculated. Despite temporary reverses, our army and our navy are bravely beating off enemy attacks along the whole front, inflicting heavy losses, while our country—our whole country—has organized itself into a single fighting camp in order, jointly with our army and navy, to rout the German invaders.

There was a time when our country was in a still more difficult position. Recall the year 1918, when we celebrated the first anniversary of the October Revolution. At that time three-quarters of our country was in the hands of foreign interventionists. We had temporarily lost the Ukraine, the Caucasus, Central Asia, the Urals, Siberia, and the Far East. We had no allies, we had no Red Army—we had only just begun to create it—and we experienced a shortage of bread, a shortage of arms, a shortage of equipment.

At that time 14 states were arrayed against our country, but we did not become despondent or downhearted. In the midst of the conflagration of war we organized the Red Army and converted our country into a military camp. The spirit of the great Lenin inspired us at that time for the war against the interventionists.

And what happened? We defeated the interventionists, regained all our lost territories and achieved victory.

Today our country is in a far better position than it was 23 years ago. Today it is many times richer in industry, food and raw materials. Today we have allies who jointly with us form a united front against the German invaders. Today we enjoy the sympathy and support of all the peoples of Europe fallen under the yoke of Fascist tyranny. Today we have a splendid army and a splen-

did navy, defending the freedom and independence of our country with their lives. We experience no serious shortage either of food or of arms or equipment. . . .

Is it possible, then, to doubt that we can and must gain victory over the German invaders? The enemy is not as strong as some terror-stricken pseudo-intellectuals picture him. The devil is not as terrible as he is painted. Who can deny that our Red Army has more than once put the much-vaunted German troops to panicky flight? . . .

Comrades, Red Army and Red Navy men, commanders and political instructors, men and women guerrillas!

The whole world is looking to you as a force capable of destroying the brigand hordes of German invaders. The enslaved peoples of Europe under the yoke of the German invaders are looking to you as their liberators. A great mission of liberation has fallen to your lot.

Be worthy of this mission! The war you are waging is a war of liberation, a just war. Let the heroic images of our great ancestors . . . inspire you in this war!

Let the victorious banner of the great Lenin fly over your heads!

Utter destruction to the German invaders!

Death to the German armies of occupation!

Long live our glorious motherland, her freedom and her independence!

Under the banner of Lenin—onward to victory!

THE CONSEQUENCES

The troops went straight from Red Square to the front. The army held out, and in the north the Germans were brought to a halt. Stalin called for a counterattack despite doubts from his commanders.

On December 5 the Red Army commenced the strategic counteroffensive operation in a period known as the Winter Campaign, pushing the Germans away from the capital. By early January they had been forced back over 150 miles. By staging a series of repetitive offensives, often using fresh soldiers, Stalin proved that the blitzkrieg could be thwarted. His approach set an example for troops throughout the world.

Hitler's decision to invade the Soviet Union was probably the single most catastrophic error in military judgment in twentieth-century history. But the Soviet Union's doubted defense was not without its cost: The death toll from World War II, civilian and military, is thought to have exceeded 23 million, or 14 percent of its population.

Lenin's words, and tireless behind-the-scenes machinations, ultimately sparked the October Revolution of 1917. This event overthrew the Russian provisional government and placed the Bolsheviks, with Lenin and Stalin as leaders, in power.

OTHER NOTABLE LINES

Some twenty years before the start of World War II, the First World War raged. Hundreds of thousands of Russian peasants were drafted, food shortages were common, and the time was ripe for revolt. In February 1917 the Social Democratic Worker's Party helped to overthrow tsarist rule. Two months later, crowds thronged the streets of St. Petersburg to welcome home the party's Bolshevik faction leader Vladimir Lenin, long exiled in Europe.

The following day, Lenin outlined ten action points for the party in his "April Theses." These goals included ending the war, rejecting the provisional government, redistributing land, claiming power for workers, and a call to bring Russia fully into the Communist fold:

"The masses must be made to see that the Soviets of Workers' Deputies are the only possible form of revolutionary government, and that therefore our task is, as long as this [provisional] government yields to the influence of the bourgeoisie, to present a patient, systematic, and persistent explanation of the errors of their tactics, an explanation especially adapted to the practical needs of the masses.

"As long as we are in the minority, we carry on the work of criticizing and exposing errors and at the same time we preach the necessity of transferring the entire state power to the Soviets of Workers' Deputies, so that the people may overcome their mistakes by experience."

1941

A Date Which Will Live in Infamy

Franklin Delano Roosevelt

(1882–1945)

When American radar operators spotted a large formation of unknown airplanes approaching the naval base at Pearl Harbor, Hawaii, they were right to be alarmed. World War II was raging in Europe, and things in the Pacific were heating up. Diplomats and code breakers had been warning for months that Japan might break the peace with the United States and that the expansionist Japanese military might attempt a surprise attack.

But when the sighting was reported to the radar information center at Fort Shafter, the duty officer told the operators not to worry. A flight of friendly bombers was expected that day and was the only plausible explanation for the unusual blip on the radar screens. Surely, the Japanese, for all their daring, would never risk so bold a strike so far from their own territory.

Hours later that same duty officer watched in horror as hundreds of Japanese fighters and dive bombers swarmed out of the summer sky to devastate the lines of U.S. ships that lay anchored in the harbor. By the end of the attack, more than 2,000 U.S. servicemen had lost their lives.

The next day, President Franklin Delano Roosevelt addressed the U.S. Congress, giving a speech that would etch itself forever onto America's national consciousness.

THE SPEECH

Mr. Vice President, and Mr. Speaker, and Members of the Senate and House of Representatives:

Yesterday, December 7, 1941—a date which will live in infamy—the United States of America was suddenly and deliberately attacked by naval and air forces of the Empire of Japan.

The United States was at peace with that nation and, at the solicitation of Japan, was still in conversation with its government and its emperor looking toward the maintenance of peace in the Pacific. Indeed, one hour after Japanese air squadrons had commenced bombing in the American Island of Oahu, the Japanese ambassador to the United States and his colleague delivered to our secretary of state a formal reply to a recent American message. And while this reply stated that it seemed useless to continue the existing diplomatic negotiations, it contained no threat or hint of war or of armed attack.

It will be recorded that the distance of Hawaii from Japan makes it obvious that the attack was deliberately planned many days or even weeks ago. During the intervening time the Japanese government has deliberately sought to deceive the United States by false statements and expressions of hope for continued peace.

The attack yesterday on the Hawaiian Islands has caused severe damage to American naval and military forces. I regret to tell you that very many American lives have been lost. In addition American ships have been reported torpedoed on the high seas between San Francisco and Honolulu.

Yesterday the Japanese government also launched an attack against Malaya.

Last night Japanese forces attacked Hong Kong.

Last night Japanese forces attacked Guam.

Last night Japanese forces attacked the Philippine Islands.

Last night the Japanese attacked Wake Island. And this morning the Japanese attacked Midway Island.

Japan has, therefore, undertaken a surprise offensive extending throughout the Pacific area. The facts of yesterday and today speak for themselves. The people of the United States have already formed their opinions and well understand the implications to the very life and safety of our nation.

As commander in chief of the army and navy, I have directed that all measures be taken for our defense.

But always will our whole nation remember the character of the onslaught against us.

No matter how long it may take us to overcome this premeditated invasion, the American people in their righteous might will win through to absolute victory. I believe that I interpret the will of the Congress and of the people when I assert that we will not only defend ourselves to the uttermost but will make it very certain that this form of treachery shall never again endanger us.

Hostilities exist. There is no blinking at the fact that our people, our territory, and our interests are in grave danger.

With confidence in our armed forces—with the unbounding determination of our people—we will gain the inevitable triumph, so help us God.

I ask that the Congress declare that since the unprovoked and dastardly attack by Japan on Sunday, December 7, 1941, a state of war has existed between the United States and the Japanese empire.

THE CONSEQUENCES

By attacking Pearl Harbor, Japan had won a stunning tactical victory. At the same time, however, the country had ensured its own inevitable defeat. The United States had been unwilling to join the war. Isolationist sentiment was widespread and powerful. But confronted with the photographs of burning battleships and the lists of dead sailors, the previously unwilling populace hurled itself into battle.

Roosevelt's speech was stern and simple—a perfect expression of a newfound national resolve. America's "righteous might," he said, and "unbounding determination" would bring "absolute victory."

And though the fight was hard, the balance soon began to swing America's way. At the Battle of Midway, six months later, American airmen had their revenge, crippling the Japanese carrier fleet. U.S. Marines began to push back the Japanese advances in the Pacific. Meanwhile, deep in rural New Mexico, a group of scientists was building the weapon that would repay the debt of Pearl Harbor a thousandfold.

In August 1945 the Americans dropped an atom bomb on the Japanese city of Hiroshima, followed soon after by another, on Nagasaki. Days later Japan offered an unconditional surrender.

OTHER NOTABLE LINES

J. Robert Oppenheimer has the ambiguous distinction of being remembered in history as the father of the atom bomb. He was a brilliant scientist and an ambitious man. He was deeply curious about whether the bomb could be made to work and was pleased when it did.

But he was not a fool. He knew that the device that he and his team at Los Alamos had put together was something both miraculous and awful. In a television broadcast years later, he recalled how he had felt as he watched the first successful bomb test—a quote that would go down in history:

"We knew the world would not be the same. A few people laughed, a few people cried, most people were silent. I remembered the line from the Hindu scripture, the Bhagavad-Gita: 'Now, I am become Death, the destroyer of worlds.' I suppose we all thought that one way or another."

1947

A Tryst with Destiny

Jawaharlal Nehru

(1889–1964)

By the beginning of the 1940s, Britain had realized that its days of empire in India were coming to an end. A tiny island nation, bankrupted by World War II, could no longer hope to control a subcontinent of a quarter of a billion people.

And those countless millions were becoming ever more difficult to rule. Mohandas Gandhi's nonviolent resistance had embarrassed the British overlords. More dangerous yet, the old imperial glue that had joined India's diverse peoples together was coming rapidly unstuck, as Muslims and Hindus clashed violently in the streets.

So in 1947 a new British viceroy, the dashing Admiral Lord Louis Mountbatten, arrived in Delhi to get Britain out of India. Five months later the deed was done and India declared independence.

The first man to try to lead this newly created nation was Jawaharlal Nehru, an aristocratic politician and a veteran of India's long struggle for freedom. Nehru was a fierce believer in Indian independence, but he was also, in many respects, every bit the elegant English gentleman, educated at Harrow and Cambridge and trained in law at London's elite Inner Temple. On the night of August 14, as his country prepared for independence, Nehru made the following speech.

THE SPEECH

Long years ago we made a tryst with destiny, and now the time comes when we shall redeem our pledge, not wholly or in full measure, but very substantially.

At the stroke of the midnight hour, when the world sleeps, India will awake to life and freedom. A moment comes, which comes but rarely in history, when we step out from the old to the new, when an age ends, and when the soul of a nation, long suppressed, finds utterance. . . .

The appointed day has come—the day appointed by destiny—and India stands forth again, after long slumber and struggle, awake, vital, free and independent. The past clings onto us still in some measure and we have to do much before we redeem the pledges we have so often taken. Yet the turning point is past, and history begins anew for us, the history which we shall live and act and others will write about.

It is a fateful moment for us in India, for all Asia and for the world. A new star rises, the star of freedom in the east, a new hope comes into being, a vision long cherished materializes. May the star never set and that hope never be betrayed!

We rejoice in that freedom, even though clouds surround us, and many of our people are sorrow-stricken and difficult problems encompass us. But freedom brings responsibilities and burdens and we have to face them in the spirit of a free and disciplined people. . . .

We are citizens of a great country, on the verge of bold advance, and we have to live up to that high standard. All of us, to whatever religion we may belong, are equally the children of India with equal rights, privileges, and obligations. We cannot encourage communalism or narrow-mindedness, for no nation can be great whose people are narrow in thought or in action.

To the nations and peoples of the world we send greetings and pledge ourselves to cooperate with them in furthering peace, freedom and democracy.

And to India, our much-loved motherland, the ancient, the eternal and the ever-new, we pay our reverent homage and we bind ourselves afresh to her service. Jai Hind [Victory to India]!

THE CONSEQUENCES

Amid the "trysts with destiny" and "stars of freedom," Nehru had carefully sounded a more cautious note, warning of the "difficult problems" that lay ahead. Sadly, his fears were fully realized.

The same act of Parliament that gave India independence had also, at the urging of the powerful Muslim League, divided the old British dominion into two new countries: Hindu India and Muslim Pakistan.

On the day of partition, millions of refugees crossed the newly drawn borders. As they passed through hostile communities, unrest became a full-blown civil war, with massacres carried out on both sides. Hundreds of thousands were killed.

However, more than half a century later, India is emerging from poverty to become one of the world's major democratic powers. Despite the pitfalls and problems and the continuing tensions with Pakistan, Nehru's idealistic vision of India is slowly being fulfilled.

1949

The Chinese People Have Stood Up

Mao Zedong

(1893–1976)

Mao Zedong was born in 1893 in a remote farming community in Hunan Province, China, the only son of the family's three children to survive infancy. His father, strict and stern, enrolled him in school at age eight, and the young Mao loved reading, writing, and poetry. As a young man, he abandoned farming for more schooling in the province's capital city of Changsha, where he became swept up in revolutionary fervor and a desire to replace the ruling dynasty with a modern republic.

After the revolution, Mao became heavily influenced by the Communist writings of Karl Marx and founded a branch of the Communist party in Changsha. He was dedicated now to a new revolution, and he would spend the next 28 years in a violent struggle to remake Chinese society in Marx's image. In 1949 "Chairman Mao" stood in Tiananmen Square, Beijing, and proclaimed victory for the newly minted People's Republic of China. In a speech given just a few days prior, he outlines the driving forces of the new government.

THE SPEECH

Fellow Delegates, we are all convinced that our work will go down in the history of mankind, demonstrating that the Chinese people, comprising one quarter of humanity, have now stood up. The Chinese have always been a great, courageous, and industrious nation; it is only in modern times that they have fallen behind. And that was due entirely to oppression and exploitation by foreign imperialism and domestic reactionary governments. . . . We have closed our ranks and defeated both domestic and foreign oppressors through the People's War of Liberation and the great people's revolution, and now we are proclaiming the founding of the People's Republic of China. . . . Ours will no longer be a nation subject to insult and humiliation. We have stood up. . . .

Our revolutionary work is not completed, the People's War of Liberation and the people's revolutionary movement are still forging ahead and we must keep up our efforts. The imperialists and the domestic reactionaries will certainly not take their defeat lying down; they will fight to the last ditch. After there is peace and order throughout the country, they are sure to engage in sabotage and create disturbances . . . and under no circumstances must we relax our vigilance. . . .

The people's democratic dictatorship and solidarity with our foreign friends will enable us to accomplish our work of construction rapidly. We are already confronted with the task of nationwide economic construction. We have very favorable conditions: a population of 475 million people and a territory of 9,600,000 square kilometers. There are indeed difficulties ahead, and a great many too. . . . The Chinese people have rich experience in overcoming difficulties. . . .

Our national defense will be consolidated and no imperialists will ever again be allowed to invade our land. Our people's armed forces must be maintained and developed with the heroic and steeled People's Liberation Army as the foundation. We will have not only a powerful army but also a powerful air force and a powerful navy.

Let the domestic and foreign reactionaries tremble before us! Let them say we are no good at this and no good at that. By our own indomitable efforts we the Chinese people will unswervingly reach our goal. . . .

Hail the victory of the People's War of Liberation and the people's revolution!

Hail the founding of the People's Republic of China!

THE CONSEQUENCES

From the beginning, Mao had high expectations for his country, now jubilant after three decades of civil war and Japanese aggression. His plans to root out adversaries from within the country, catch up to the world economically, and militarily dominate any aggressors would be imposed systematically and repeatedly throughout his 27 years in power. Within the first two years of his rule, Mao had executed some 700,000 people said to be counter-revolutionaries and sent many more to labor camps. As he had said as leader of his Red Army in 1938, "political power grows out of the barrel of a gun."

Mao's economic ideas would transform the country from small farming communities to group cooperatives and finally, during the disastrous Great Leap Forward of 1958, to village communes. The push to raise capital through agricultural and steel exports, combined with drought, led to the deaths of millions through starvation, execution, and suicide. However, the 1950s saw some gains—factories were producing goods, and agricultural production had increased. Mao remained in power as "Great Leader" of the nation until his death in 1976.

Mao's reforms dragged China into the twentieth century and lie at the root of its current wealth, but the power that grew from the gun could not loosen its grip on violence. Today China boasts the world's second-largest economy behind the United States, but millions of Chinese have died, become imprisoned, tortured, and intimidated along the path of progress.

1960

Wind of Change

Harold Macmillan

(1894–1986)

In the decades following World War II, it became clear that the age of empire was over. India was independent. Southeast Asia had launched its own struggle against colonialism. And in Africa, almost all of which was controlled by one of the European powers, a new generation of educated black nationalists was coming to the fore, demanding freedom after centuries of white rule.

Through the 1950s and 1960s, more and more of these African countries got their way. The great swaths of British pink that covered the continent on classroom maps gave way to a patchwork of newly independent nations.

In 1960, as this movement was at its height, the British prime minister, Harold Macmillan, traveled to South Africa. The republic had been independent since 1931, but for the substantial black majority, this had not led to any sort of liberation. Instead, a white colonial elite enforced a strict segregationist policy of apartheid (meaning "separateness") that subjected the country's black citizens to repressive legalized discrimination.

Arriving in Cape Town, Macmillan addressed a state that was still deeply wedded to the racist legacy of the past. His task was to open its eyes to the new reality of the present.

THE SPEECH

Ever since the break-up of the Roman Empire, one of the constant facts of political life in Europe has been the emergence of independent nations. They have come into existence over the centuries in different forms, different kinds of government, but all have been inspired by a deep, keen feeling of nationalism, which has grown as the nations have grown. . . .

Today the same thing is happening in Africa, and the most striking of all the impressions I have formed since I left London a month ago is of the strength of this African national consciousness. In different places it takes different forms, but it is happening everywhere.

The wind of change is blowing through this continent, and whether we like it or not, this growth of national consciousness is a political fact. We must all accept it as a fact, and our national policies must take account of it.

Well, you understand this better than anyone, you are sprung from Europe, the home of nationalism, here in Africa you have yourselves created a free nation. A new nation. Indeed in the history of our times yours will be recorded as the first of the African nationalists. This tide of national consciousness which is now rising in Africa, is a fact, for which both you and we, and the other nations of the western world are ultimately responsible.

For its causes are to be found in the achievements of western civilization, in the pushing forwards of the frontiers of knowledge, the applying of science to the service of human needs, in the expanding of food production, in the speeding and multiplying of the means of communication, and perhaps above all and more than anything else in the spread of education.

As I have said, the growth of national consciousness in Africa is a political fact, and we must accept it as such. That means, I would judge, that we've got to come to terms with it. I sincerely believe that if we cannot do so we may imperil the precarious balance between the East and West on which the peace of the world depends.

THE CONSEQUENCES

Macmillan was a British Conservative politician of the old school, educated at Eton, steeped in the mannerisms of the traditional ruling class. But although his message was delivered with typical patrician charm, it concealed a severe rebuke. As Douglas Hurd, a former Conservative foreign secretary, later wrote, when Macmillan said, "Of course, you understand this better than anyone," he really meant: "You need to understand this more than anyone, but I doubt you do."

South Africa, it was strongly implied, had fallen behind the times. Not only that—by failing to provide a good example of Western values in action, it risked driving the new nations of Africa toward the chilly embrace of the Soviet bloc and disastrously upsetting the precarious balance of Cold War power.

Sadly, South Africa refused to heed Macmillan's warning. Apartheid remained central to the country's policy for a further three decades, leaving it economically backward and politically isolated. But Macmillan's speech did send out an important signal to the rest of Africa. Despite the old bonds of friendship between the two nations, Britain would not stand with South Africa in resisting the "wind of change."

1961

Inaugural Address

John F. Kennedy

(1917–1963)

John Fitzgerald Kennedy certainly overcame his share of challenges on his way to the U.S. presidency. When he was a naval officer in World War II, his patrol boat was sunk by a Japanese destroyer; he floated in the sea for three days before he was saved. As a young congressman, he was dogged by illness (a rare endocrine disorder called Addison's Disease); steroid injections finally saved his career.

Far more formidable obstacles lay in wait simply by virtue of his birth. For one thing, at age 43 he was an extraordinarily young presidential candidate. And even worse, he was Catholic. With the Cold War reaching a climax, any ill-defined sense that Kennedy was in some way un-American could have been fatal.

But by the narrowest of margins, Kennedy won the

presidential election of 1960. Now he had to win over the American people. Coming into a political sphere dominated by aged white Protestants (President Eisenhower, the incumbent, was the oldest man ever to have held the office), Kennedy, in his inaugural address, took his perceived weaknesses and turned them into strengths, presenting himself as part of a fresh new generation.

THE SPEECH

Fellow citizens:

We observe today not a victory of party but a celebration of freedom—symbolizing an end as well as a beginning—signifying renewal as well as change. For I have sworn before you and Almighty God the same solemn oath our forebears prescribed nearly a century and three-quarters ago.

The world is very different now. For man holds in his mortal hands the power to abolish all forms of human poverty and all forms of human life. And yet the same revolutionary beliefs for which our forebears fought are still at issue around the globe—the belief that the rights of man come not from the generosity of the state but from the hand of God.

We dare not forget today that we are the heirs of that first revolution. Let the word go forth from this time and place, to friend and foe alike, that the torch has been passed to a new generation of Americans—born in this century, tempered by war, disciplined by a hard and bitter peace, proud of our ancient heritage—and unwilling to witness or permit the slow undoing of those human rights to which this nation has always been committed, and to which we are committed today at home and around the world.

Let every nation know, whether it wishes us well or ill, that we shall pay any price, bear any burden, meet any hardship, support any friend, oppose any foe to assure the survival and the success of liberty. . . .

This much we pledge—and more.

To those old allies whose cultural and spiritual origins we share, we pledge the loyalty of faithful friends . . .

To those new states whom we welcome to the ranks of the free, we pledge our word that one form of colonial control shall not have passed away merely to be replaced by a far more iron tyranny . . .

To those people in the huts and villages of half the globe struggling to break the bonds of mass misery, we pledge our best efforts to help them help themselves, for whatever period is required . . . If a free society cannot help the many who are poor, it cannot save the few who are rich.

To our sister republics south of our border, we offer a special pledge—to convert our good words into good deeds—in a new alliance for progress—to assist free men and free governments in casting off the chains of poverty . . .

To that world assembly of sovereign states, the United Nations, our last best hope in an age where the instruments of war have far outpaced the instruments of peace, we renew our pledge of support . . .

Finally, to those nations who would make themselves our adversary, we offer not a pledge but a request: that both sides begin anew the quest for peace, before the dark powers of destruction unleashed by science engulf all humanity in planned or accidental self-destruction. . . .

In the long history of the world, only a few generations have been granted the role of defending freedom in its hour of maximum danger. I do not shrink from this responsibility—I welcome it. I do not believe that any of us would exchange places with any other people or any other generation. The energy, the faith, the devotion which we bring to this endeavor will light our country and all who serve it—and the glow from that fire can truly light the world.

And so, my fellow Americans: ask not what your country can do for you—ask what you can do for your country.

My fellow citizens of the world: ask not what America will do for you, but what together we can do for the freedom of man.

THE CONSEQUENCES

Kennedy came to power at a time of huge global challenges. The Cold War had reached new and perilous heights. In June 1961 Kennedy endured a difficult meeting with his Soviet counterpart Nikita Khruschev, who dominated the young president, warning that communism would "bury" the capitalist West.

Soon construction started on the Berlin Wall, separating capitalist West Berlin from the Soviet East. The U.S.-sponsored Bay of Pigs invasion of Cuba was a miserable failure. A massively expanded program of Soviet missile tests escalated the nuclear arms race.

Most challenging of all was the Cuban missile crisis of 1962. For a few tense days Kennedy and Khrushchev were locked in a battle of wills over the presence of nuclear missiles just a few hundred miles off the American coast. The world seemed on the brink of an annihilating nuclear war.

In those dark days, Kennedy's speech stood as a shining declaration of intent—a bold statement that the United States of America had what it took to overcome all challenges. For 1,037 days, until he was assassinated by Lee Harvey Oswald in 1963, Kennedy led his nation through one of the toughest periods in American history. He remains among the country's most celebrated presidents.

OTHER NOTABLE LINES

Kennedy's embrace of technological and scientific advances further strengthened his legacy as president of "a new generation of Americans." In a 1962 address at Rice University in Houston, he pledged that the United States would send a man to the moon that decade, saying, "We choose to go to the moon . . . not because [it is] easy, but because [it is] hard." On July 20, 1969, the world held its breath as a fragile craft holding two American astronauts approached the barren surface of Earth's moon. At last the Eagle lander touched down on the dry rock. From the inside of the lunar module, Neil Armstrong radioed back to NASA in Texas. "Houston, Tranquillity Base here. The Eagle has landed."

There were still hours of preparation before the astronauts could open the Eagle's hatch. But at last, on July 21, Neil Armstrong stepped out of the cramped module into the vacuum of space. Slowly he climbed down the ladder, and as his foot touched the lunar dust, he spoke his famous words: "That's one small step for man. One giant leap for mankind."

1963

I Have a Dream

Martin Luther King, Jr.

(1929–1968)

In 1863 Abraham Lincoln's Emancipation Proclamation ended American slavery in the Unionist northern states. Two years later, with the Civil War over and the slave-owning Confederacy defeated, the captive millions toiling in the southern cotton fields looked forward to a new dawn of freedom.

For a while it looked like that dawn had come. Despite violent objection in the South, the occupying federal troops protected the black population's right to freedom and to vote.

But in 1877 the troops withdrew, leaving the South in the hands of radical Democrat politicians called the Redeemers. Black voters were prevented from registering. Racist paramilitaries like the Ku Klux Klan formed lynch mobs. Before long a string of segregation laws had designated whites-only train carriages, cafés, drinking fountains, and waiting rooms.

Into this apartheid United States of America, Martin Luther King, Jr., was born. As the son of a respected Baptist preacher and civil rights activist, it was no surprise when young Martin announced an "inner urge" to "serve God and humanity." By 1955 he had a doctorate in theology and had followed his father into the Church.

By 1963 Dr. King, with his ringing preacher's tones and knack for rhetoric, had become a leader of the growing civil rights movement, demanding an end to segregation and legal discrimination. So it was that he found himself, late that summer, facing a vast crowd in Washington, D.C., where, under the shadow of the Lincoln Memorial, he gave the following extraordinary speech.

THE SPEECH

Five score years ago, a great American, in whose symbolic shadow we stand today, signed the Emancipation Proclamation. This momentous decree came as a great beacon light of hope to millions of Negro slaves who had been seared in the flames of withering injustice. It came as a joyous daybreak to end the long night of their captivity.

But one hundred years later, the Negro still is not free. One hundred years later, the life of the Negro is still sadly crippled by the manacles of segregation and the chains of discrimination . . . And so we've come here today to dramatize a shameful condition. . . .

[King continued with his prepared speech, and he reached his intended conclusion. As King was about to sit

down, the singer Mahalia Jackson called to him from the crowd: "Tell them about your dream, Martin." Hearing her, King began to extemporize, and it is at this point that the speech comes alive.]

Let us not wallow in the valley of despair, I say to you today, my friends.

And so even though we face the difficulties of today and tomorrow, I still have a dream. It is a dream deeply rooted in the American dream.

I have a dream that one day this nation will rise up and live out the true meaning of its creed: "We hold these truths to be self-evident, that all men are created equal."

I have a dream that one day on the red hills of Georgia, the sons of former slaves and the sons of former slave owners will be able to sit down together at the table of brotherhood.

I have a dream that one day even the state of Mississippi, a state sweltering with the heat of injustice, sweltering with the heat of oppression, will be transformed into an oasis of freedom and justice.

I have a dream that my four little children will one day live in a nation where they will not be judged by the color of their skin but by the content of their character.

I have a dream today!

I a dream that one day, down in Alabama, with its vicious racists, with its governor having his lips dripping with the words of "interposition" and "nullification"—one day right there in Alabama little black boys and black girls will be able to join hands with little white boys and white girls as sisters and brothers.

I have a dream today!

I have a dream that one day every valley shall be exalted, and every hill and mountain shall be made low, the rough places will be made plain, and the crooked places will be made straight; "and the glory of the Lord shall be revealed and all flesh shall see it together."

This is our hope, and this is the faith that I go back to the South with.

With this faith, we will be able to hew out of the mountain of despair a stone of hope. With this faith, we will be able to transform the jangling discords of our nation into a beautiful symphony of brotherhood. With this faith, we will be able to work together, to pray together, to struggle together, to go to jail together, to stand up for freedom together, knowing that we will be free one day.

And this will be the day—this will be the day when all of God's children will be able to sing with new meaning:

My country 'tis of thee, sweet land of liberty, of thee I sing.

Land where my fathers died, land of the Pilgrim's pride, From every mountainside, let freedom ring!

And if America is to be a great nation, this must become true.

And so let freedom ring from the prodigious hilltops of New Hampshire.

Let freedom ring from the mighty mountains of New York.

Let freedom ring from the heightening Alleghenies of Pennsylvania.

Let freedom ring from the snowcapped Rockies of Colorado.

Let freedom ring from the curvaceous slopes of California.

But not only that:

Let freedom ring from Stone Mountain of Georgia.

Let freedom ring from Lookout Mountain of Tennessee.

Let freedom ring from every hill and molehill of Mississippi.

From every mountainside, let freedom ring.

And when this happens, when we allow freedom to ring, when we let it ring from every village and every hamlet, from every state and every city, we will be able to speed up that day when all of God's children, black men and white men, Jews and Gentiles, Protestants and Catholics, will be able to join hands and sing in the words of the old Negro spiritual:

Free at last! Free at last!

Thank God Almighty, we are free at last!

THE CONSEQUENCES

Dr. King's speech was a milestone in America's struggle for civil rights. His fiery words, which blended intellectual argument, biblical rhetoric, and patriotic exhortation ("let freedom ring" turns the words "My Country 'Tis of Thee" into something that is almost a prayer), gave new heart to the advocates of black equality.

Just as important, it forced the politicians in Washington to sit up and take notice. In 1964 the U.S. government finally passed the Civil Rights Act, officially ending segregation. A year later the Voting Rights Act ended the disenfranchisement of African Americans.

But this was not the end of the struggle. Discrimination was still rife. Many black activists, disillusioned, were rejecting King's nonviolent precepts in favor of a more militant kind of struggle.

By 1968 King's influence was on the wane, but he remained optimistic. "It doesn't matter with me now," he said in a speech to his followers, "because I've been to the mountaintop and I've seen the Promised Land. I may not get there with you. But I want you to know tonight, that we, as a people, will get to the Promised Land."

The next day, standing on the balcony of a Memphis hotel, Martin Luther King, Jr., was shot and killed by a white segregationist. He was 39 years old.

OTHER NOTABLE LINES

While Martin Luther King, Jr., sought equality for African Americans through nonviolent protest, a more militant movement was growing in the shadows—the Nation of Islam. Its most famous figurehead was Malcolm X.

Born in Nebraska as Malcolm Little, he reinvented himself as a black nationalist. The X was a symbol for his lost African name, stolen from his ancestors by their slavemasters.

Malcolm X forcefully denounced King's peaceful campaigns. "Revolution is bloody," he once said. But by 1964 he had started to soften his position. He rejected the Nation of Islam and started to advocate political rather than militant activism.

In perhaps his most famous speech, Malcolm X uses straightforward language—and draws on his understanding of the other, aggressive approach to change:

"If we don't do something real soon, I think you'll have to agree that we're going to be forced either to use the ballot or the bullet. It's one or the other in 1964. It isn't that time is running out—time has run out!"

In speaking about bullets, Malcolm X reportedly said, "If the white people realize what the alternative is, perhaps they will be more willing to hear Dr. King." In 1965 the Voting Rights Act ended all legal disenfranchisement of African Americans. The ballot, not the bullet, would be the preferred weapon during the ongoing struggle for equality.

1974

Today I Am an Inquisitor

Barbara Jordan

(1936–1996)

Barbara Jordan's political career began in the Texas senate, her law degree from Boston University a stepping stone to public service. Politics was an easy fit for the high-achieving, gifted orator and debater. Jordan had grown up in the Jim Crow era, the youngest daughter of a Baptist minister, and was determined to be part of the social change sweeping through America in the 1960s. In 1972 she took her seat as representative of Texas—the first African-American woman elected from a southern state.

Jordan's first term in office coincided with a presidency in turmoil. What began as a break-in gone wrong in an office complex called the Watergate had snowballed into a political spying scandal and an investigation into President Richard Nixon's role in the sabotage. As a member of the House Judiciary Committee, she found herself responsible for deciding whether impeachment should proceed. Jordan, ever the lawyer, based her opinion on precedent, quoting from documents early founders had used to push for the ratification of the Constitution in 1788.

THE SPEECH

Today I am an inquisitor. . . . My faith in the Constitution is whole, it is complete, it is total. I am not going to sit here and be an idle spectator to the diminution, the subversion, the destruction of the Constitution. . . .

We know the nature of impeachment. We have been talking about it awhile now. "It is chiefly designed for the president and his high ministers" to somehow be called into account. It is designed to "bridle" the executive if he engages in excesses. "It is designed as a method of national inquest into the public men." ["The Federalist Papers," 1788] . . .

This morning, in a discussion of the evidence, we were told that the evidence which purports to support the allegations of misuse of the CIA by the president is thin. We are told that that evidence is insufficient. What that recital of the evidence this morning did not include is what the president did know on June 23, 1972. The president did know that it was Republican money, that it was money from the Committee for the Re-Election of the President, which was found in the possession of one of the burglars arrested on June 17.

What the president did know on the 23rd of June was the prior activities of E. Howard Hunt, which included his participation in the break-in of Daniel Ellsberg's psychiatrist, which included Howard Hunt's participation in the Dita Beard ITT affair, which included Howard Hunt's fabrication of cables designed to discredit the Kennedy administration.

We were further cautioned today that perhaps these proceedings ought to be delayed because certainly there would be new evidence forthcoming from the president of the United States. . . . The committee subpoena is outstanding, and if the president wants to supply that material, the committee sits here.

The fact is that yesterday, the American people waited with great anxiety for eight hours, not knowing whether their president would obey an order of the Supreme Court of the United States.

At this point I would like to juxtapose a few of the impeachment criteria with some of the actions the president has engaged in.

Impeachment criteria: James Madison, from the Virginia ratification convention. "If the president be connected in any suspicious manner with any person and there be grounds to believe that he will shelter him, he may be impeached."

We have heard time and time again that the evidence reflects the payment to the defendants [of] money. The president had knowledge that these funds were being paid and that these were funds collected for the 1972 presidential campaign. We know that the president met with Mr. Henry Petersen 27 times to discuss matters related to Watergate and immediately thereafter met with the very persons who were implicated in the information Mr. Petersen was receiving. The words are "if the president be connected in any suspicious manner with any person and there be grounds to believe that he will shelter that person, he may be impeached." . . .

[Jordan continues to compare President Nixon's actions with those considered impeachable according to early documents from the nation's founding. She closes with words of James Madison at the Constitutional Convention, 1788.]

The Constitution charges the president with the task of taking care that the laws be faithfully executed, and yet the president has counseled his aides to commit perjury, willfully disregard the secrecy of grand jury proceedings, conceal surreptitious entry, attempt to compromise a federal judge while publicly displaying his cooperation with the processes of criminal justice.

"A president is impeachable if he attempts to subvert the Constitution."

If the impeachment provision in the Constitution of the United States will not reach the offenses charged here, then perhaps that eighteenth-century Constitution should be abandoned to a twentieth-century paper shredder.

Has the president committed offenses and planned and directed and acquiesced in a course of conduct which the Constitution will not tolerate? That is the question. We know that. We know the question. We should now forthwith proceed to answer the question. It is reason, and not passion, which must guide our deliberations, guide our debate, and guide our decision.

THE CONSEQUENCES

Jordan's address, beamed in prime time to televisions across the nation, clearly laid the case for impeachment and separated impeachment from party politics. Lawmakers and ordinary citizens alike were moved by her sense of justice, rightness, and outrage.

The committee voted to commence impeachment proceedings, though Nixon resigned before he could be remove from office. Barbara Jordan was catapulted to the national stage and, in 1976, was asked to speak at the Democratic National Convention, the first woman and the first African American to do so.

In 1979 Barbara Jordan declined to seek another term of office and instead began her second career as professor of public affairs and ethics at the University of Texas. Jordan influenced and inspired students for 17 years, even as her health declined. She had been diagnosed with multiple sclerosis in her first term of Congress and died in 1996.

1980

The Lady's Not for Turning

Margaret Thatcher

(1925–)

In the British general election of 1979, a greengrocer's daughter from Lincolnshire made history by becoming the UK's first female prime minister. Her name was Margaret Thatcher, and she was a new kind of Conservative politician. She came from a modest background, brought up in a flat above her family's shop—an upbringing that gave her a lifelong respect for what might have been called bourgeois values: self-reliance, patriotism, entrepreneurialism.

But when Thatcher came to power after the financial crises of the 1970s, Britain was stripped of its colonies, rocked by recession and suffering from severe inflation. To reverse this, Thatcher introduced harsh fiscal measures aimed at reducing inflation. However, this caused rising unemployment and popular discontent, which then led to widespread media speculation about a possible "U-turn." Characteristically, at the 1980 Conservative Party conference, Thatcher took the opportunity to address the doubters head-on.

THE SPEECH

It is sometimes said that because of our past we, as a people, expect too much and set our sights too high. That is not the way I see it. Rather it seems to me that throughout my life in politics our ambitions have steadily shrunk. Our response to disappointment has not been to lengthen our stride but to shorten the distance to be covered. But with confidence in ourselves and in our future what a nation we could be!

Thatcher next lists her party's economic accomplishments;

But all this will avail us little unless we achieve our prime economic objective—the defeat of inflation. Inflation destroys nations and societies as surely as invading armies do. Inflation is the parent of unemployment. It is the unseen robber of those who have saved.

. . . Some people talk as if control of the money supply [to combat inflation] was a revolutionary policy. Yet it was an essential condition for the recovery of much of continental Europe. Those countries knew what was required for economic stability. . . .

Today, after many years of monetary self-discipline, they have stable, prosperous economies better able than ours to withstand the buffeting of world recession.

[European leaders ask:] "Has Britain the courage and resolve to sustain the discipline for long enough to break through to success?"

Yes, Mr. Chairman, we have, and we shall. This Government are determined to stay with the policy and see it through to its conclusion. That is what marks this administration as one of the truly radical ministries of post-war Britain. Inflation is falling and should continue to fall.

Meanwhile we are not heedless of the hardships and worries that accompany the conquest of inflation. Foremost among these is unemployment. Today our country has more than 2 million unemployed. Now you can try to soften that figure in a dozen ways. . . . But when all that has been said, the fact remains that the level of unemployment in our country today is a human tragedy. . . . The waste of a country's most precious assets—the talent and energy of its people—makes it the bounden duty of Government to seek a real and lasting cure.

If spending money like water was the answer to our country's problems, we would have no problems now. If ever a nation has spent, spent, spent and spent again, ours has. Today that dream is over. All of that money has got us nowhere, but it still has to come from somewhere. Those who urge us to relax the squeeze, to spend yet more money indiscriminately in the belief that it will help the unemployed and the small businessman are not being kind or compassionate or caring.

If our people feel that they are part of a great nation and they are prepared to will the means to keep it great, a great nation we shall be, and shall remain. So, what can stop us from achieving this? What then stands in our way? The prospect of another winter of discontent? I suppose it might. But I prefer to believe that certain lessons have been learnt from experience—that we are coming, slowly, painfully, to an autumn of understanding. And I hope that it will be followed by a winter of common sense. If it is not, we shall not be diverted from our course.

To those waiting with bated breath for that favorite media catchphrase, the "U turn", I have only one thing to say. "You turn if you want to. The lady's not for turning."

... So let us resist the blandishments of the faint hearts; let us ignore the howls and threats of the extremists; let us stand together and do our duty, and we shall not fail.

THE CONSEQUENCES

Even today, more than twenty years after she left power, Margaret Thatcher remains perhaps the most divisive prime minister in British history. To her supporters she was a visionary, singlehandedly stopping Britain's plunge toward mediocrity. To her critics she was a cold-hearted ideologue who ravaged Britain's industrial heart and brought in a new social order in which greed was the only good.

Britain's economy came through the pain of mass unemployment to reach the boom years of the 1980s before crashing again in 1991, but how much responsibility Thatcher's policies should take for either boom or bust is hotly disputed. Yet, however controversial, her economic legacy left an indelible mark on British history—the state-run industries and highly regulated markets of the 1970s were swept away, leaving today's modern capitalist society in their place.

1987

Tear Down This Wall!

Ronald Reagan

(1911–2004)

In 1937 Warner Brothers Studios in California offered a screen test to a handsome young man named Ronald Reagan. The trial was a success, and from the late 1930s to the mid-1960s, Reagan starred in a succession of modestly successful Hollywood films. He later described himself as the "Errol Flynn of the B-movies."

Although his acting career never quite brought him real stardom, it was an invaluable preparation for his future career on the greater stage of global politics. Elected governor of California in 1967, Reagan often recycled lines from his own movies in political speeches.

When he became president in 1980, Reagan found himself playing the lead in one of the twentieth century's most compelling dramas: the final decay of the Soviet

Union. A climactic moment came in 1987 in Berlin—a city divided between the communist East and the capitalist West by the notorious Berlin Wall.

New Soviet policies of openness and freedom had led to hopes that the communist regime might finally be relaxing its iron grip. In front of a crowd of thousands of West Germans, and knowing his speech was being watched in the East, Reagan issued the Soviet leader, Mikhail Gorbachev, a ringing challenge.

THE SPEECH

Our gathering today is being broadcast throughout Western Europe and North America. I understand that it is being seen and heard as well in the East. To those listening throughout Eastern Europe, I extend my warmest greetings and the goodwill of the American people. To those listening in East Berlin, a special word: Although I cannot be with you, I address my remarks to you just as surely as to those standing here before me. For I join you, as I join your fellow countrymen in the West, in this firm, this unalterable belief: Es gibt nur ein Berlin. *[There is only one Berlin.]*

Behind me stands a wall that encircles the free sectors of this city, part of a vast system of barriers that divides the entire continent of Europe. From the Baltic, south, those barriers cut across Germany in a gash of barbed wire, concrete, dog runs, and guardtowers . . . a restriction on the right to travel . . . an instrument to impose upon ordinary men and women the will of a totalitarian state.

Yet it is here in Berlin where the wall emerges most

clearly; here, cutting across your city, where the news photo and the television screen have imprinted this brutal division of a continent upon the mind of the world. Standing before the Brandenburg Gate, every man is a German, separated from his fellow men. Every man is a Berliner, forced to look upon a scar.

. . . Yet I do not come here to lament. For I find in Berlin a message of hope, even in the shadow of this wall, a message of triumph. . . .

In West Germany and here in Berlin, there took place an economic miracle. . . .

Where four decades ago there was rubble, today in West Berlin there is the greatest industrial output of any city in Germany . . . Where a city's culture seemed to have been destroyed, today there are two great universities, orchestras and an opera, countless theaters, and museums. Where there was want, today there's abundance—food, clothing, automobiles—the wonderful goods of the Ku'damm [Berlin's main commercial street]. From devastation, from utter ruin, you Berliners have, in freedom, rebuilt a city that once again ranks as one of the greatest on Earth. . . .

In the 1950s, Khrushchev predicted: "We will bury you." But in the West today, we see a free world that has achieved a level of prosperity and well-being unprecedented in all human history. In the Communist world, we see failure, technological backwardness, declining standards of health, even want of the most basic kind—too little food. Even today, the Soviet Union still cannot feed itself. After these four decades, then, there stands before the entire world one great and inescapable conclusion: Freedom leads to prosperity. Freedom replaces the ancient hatreds among the nations with comity and peace. Freedom is the victor.

And now the Soviets themselves may, in a limited way, be coming to understand the importance of freedom. We hear much from Moscow about a new policy of reform and openness. Some political prisoners have been released. Certain foreign news broadcasts are no longer being jammed. Some economic enterprises have been permitted to operate with greater freedom from state control. Are these the beginnings of profound changes in the Soviet state? Or are they token gestures, intended to raise false hopes in the West, or to strengthen the Soviet system without changing it? We welcome change and openness; for we believe that freedom and security go together, that the advance of human liberty can only strengthen the cause of world peace.

There is one sign the Soviets can make that would be unmistakable, that would advance dramatically the cause of freedom and peace. General Secretary Gorbachev, if you seek peace, if you seek prosperity for the Soviet Union and Eastern Europe, if you seek liberalization: Come here to this gate! Mr. Gorbachev, open this gate! Mr. Gorbachev, tear down this wall! . . .

As I looked out a moment ago from the Reichstag, that embodiment of German unity, I noticed words crudely spray-painted upon the wall, perhaps by a young Berliner, "This wall will fall. Beliefs become reality." Yes, across Europe, this wall will fall. For it cannot withstand faith; it cannot withstand truth. The wall cannot withstand freedom. . . .

Thank you and God bless you all.

THE CONSEQUENCES

The Berlin Wall had separated East and West Berlin since 1961. Thousands of East Berliners, desperate to escape to a better life in the West, had crossed it—some through tunnels, others by leaping out of the windows of apartment buildings, or even with the help of light aircraft or hot-air balloons.

Hundreds had died in the attempt. In the most notorious case, in 1962, an eighteen-year-old boy was shot just a few yards from the West German border. Unable to help him, Western border guards watched in horror as he bled to death from his wounds.

But in 1989, two years after Reagan's dramatic speech, a wave of popular protest on the East German side brought the hated barrier crashing down. The East Germans opened the Berlin border crossings, and within days swarms of ordinary people armed with picks and hammers had reduced much of the wall to rubble.

Symbolically, this marked the end of communist rule in Eastern Europe. Just like the wall, Soviet-backed regimes across the region crumbled. The Iron Curtain, which had split the continent for more than four decades, was lifted at last.

1990

Freedom from Fear

Aung San Suu Kyi

(1945–)

Born in Rangoon, Burma, Aung San Suu Kyi was raised by her mother after her father was assassinated by political rivals in 1947. From an early age, Suu Kyi was surrounded by people of varying backgrounds, religions, and politics, and her own mother was prominent in the newly formed Burmese government. Politically aware, and well educated in New Delhi and Oxford, she went on to work for the United Nations in New York.

Suu Kyi returned to Burma in 1988 to look after her ailing mother but soon became involved in the country's democratic movement. On August 8 of that year, a mass demonstration for democracy was violently suppressed and a new military junta seized power. In response, Suu Kyi and some fellow campaigners formed the National League for Democracy (NLD), for which they were placed under house arrest on July 20, 1989.

In 1990, facing extreme domestic and international pressure, the dictatorship was forced to call a general election. The NLD won 80 percent of the parliamentary seats, a result that the ruling generals refused to recognize.

In the same year, Suu Kyi was awarded the Sakharov Prize for Freedom of Thought and, in 1991, the Nobel Peace Prize. The following speech was given in 1991, in acceptance of the former.

THE SPEECH

It is not power that corrupts but fear. Fear of losing power corrupts those who wield it and fear of the scourge of power corrupts those who are subject to it. . . . With so close a relationship between fear and corruption it is little wonder that in any society where fear is rife corruption in all forms becomes deeply entrenched.

The effort necessary to remain uncorrupted in an environment where fear is an integral part of everyday existence is not immediately apparent to those fortunate enough to live in states governed by the rule of law. Just laws do not merely prevent corruption by meting out impartial punishment to offenders. They also help to create a society in which people can fulfill the basic requirements necessary for the preservation of human dignity without recourse to corrupt practices. Where there are no such laws, the burden of upholding the principles of justice and common decency falls on the ordinary people. It is the cumulative effect on their sustained effort and steady endurance which will change a nation where reason and conscience are warped by fear into one where legal rules exist to promote man's desire for harmony and justice while restraining the less desirable destructive traits in his nature. . . .

The wellspring of courage and endurance in the face of unbridled power is generally a firm belief in the sanctity of ethical principles combined with a historical sense that despite all setbacks the condition of man is set on an ultimate course for both spiritual and material advancement. It is his capacity for self-improvement and self-redemption which most distinguishes man from the mere brute. At the root of human responsibility is the concept of perfection, the urge to achieve it, the intelligence to find a path towards it, and the will to follow that path if not to the end at least the distance needed to rise above individual limitations and environmental impediments. It is man's vision of a world fit for rational, civilized humanity which leads him to dare and to suffer to build societies free from want and fear. Concepts such as truth, justice, and compassion cannot be dismissed as trite when these are often the only bulwarks which stand against ruthless power.

THE CONSEQUENCES

Since giving this speech, Aung San Suu Kyi has been in and out of arrest and has refused visits from her family. Drawing strength from her Buddhist faith, she remains as committed to her cause as ever. Thousands of Burmese political prisoners have drawn inspiration from her words, and though the drive to liberate all campaigners for democracy continues, international pressure has ensured degrees of freedom to many.

While she was temporarily allowed to travel in 2003, an assassination attempt was made on Suu Kyi's life as members of the Union Solidarity and Development Association (USDA), formed by the military junta, brutally attacked a convoy of vehicles. Suu Kyi reached safety, but more than 50 of her fellow NLD supporters were savagely beaten to death in what is known as the Depayin Massacre. Suu Kyi was placed under house arrest again.

Throughout 2009, diplomatic visits by the United States, coupled with pressure from various international governments and organizations, forced the Burmese government to consider the release of all its political captives. A court ruling in August set an expiry date for Suu Kyi's imprisonment.

On the evening of November 13, 2010, Aung San Suu Kyi was released from house arrest. Thousands of her supporters gathered outside her home in Rangoon to witness the removal of barricades. Many wore T-shirts emblazoned with the slogan WE STAND WITH AUNG SAN SUU KYI. Suu Kyi had been detained for 15 of the past 21 years.

1992

A Whisper of AIDS

Mary Fisher

(1948–)

When the blond mother of two approached the podium, she seemed to fit in perfectly with the assembled crowd of delegates, politicians, and their wealthy donors. She herself had served in President Gerald Ford's administration. Yet standing in the Houston Astrodome at the 1992 Republican National Convention, Mary Fisher had one thing that set her apart. Mary Fisher was HIV positive.

It was a time when the world was just waking up to the AIDS epidemic. Eighteen-year-old AIDS activist Ryan White had died just two years earlier. Earvin "Magic" Johnson had announced his HIV-positive status the year prior. To address the relative silence on the subject from the former Reagan administration and to bolster support for George H. W. Bush, Mary Fisher took the stage.

THE SPEECH

Tonight, I represent an AIDS community whose members have been reluctantly drafted from every segment of American society. . . .

This is not a distant threat. It is a present danger. . . . We have killed each other with our ignorance, our prejudice, and our silence.

We may take refuge in our stereotypes, but we cannot hide there long, because HIV asks only one thing of those it attacks. Are you human? . . . Because people with HIV . . . are human. . . . Each of them is exactly what God made: a person; not evil, deserving of our judgment; not victims, longing for our pity—people, ready for support and worthy of compassion.

My call to you, my party, is to take a public stand . . .

Tonight, HIV marches resolutely toward AIDS in more than a million American homes . . . One of the families is mine. If it is true that HIV inevitably turns to AIDS, then my children will inevitably turn to orphans. My family has been a rock of support. . . .

. . . But not all of you have been so blessed. You are HIV positive, but dare not say it. You have lost loved ones, but you dare not whisper the word AIDS. . . .

To all within the sound of my voice, I appeal: Learn with me the lessons of history and of grace, so my children will not be afraid to say the word "AIDS" when I am gone. Then, their children and yours may not need to whisper it at all. . . .

THE CONSEQUENCES

Fisher's speech silenced the noisy hall, moved many in attendance to tears, and as the *New York Times* later reported, "brought AIDS home to America." Her personal story—as a white heterosexual woman who contracted the virus in marriage—reprimanded those who viewed the disease as punishment for immoral behavior. She had come "to lift the shroud of silence which has been draped over the issue of HIV and AIDS" and to call for personal and political leadership that embraced her message: "We are a nation at risk."

The speech launched Fisher as an activist and advocate, a role she continues today. Advances in medicine mean that HIV is no longer the death sentence it once was, in part because of Republican and Democratic funding and support.

1994

Let Freedom Reign

Nelson Mandela

(1918–)

Raised by tribal royalty in a small village in South Africa's Eastern Cape province, Nelson Mandela endured years of oppression to become his country's first black president and one of the most respected statesmen of modern times.

In 1943 he joined the African National Congress (ANC), established some 30 years earlier to protest against the injustices of the apartheid regime that oppressed the country's black majority through a series of stringent segregation laws.

Mandela soon became a high-profile activist within the movement. In 1960, after 69 protesters were killed by white police in the Sharpeville Massacre, Mandela and the ANC embarked on a campaign of economic sabotage, using bombs to destroy power lines and government offices, carefully avoiding casualties.

The campaign did not last long. In 1963 Mandela was arrested and sentenced to five years for leaving the country illegally. While in prison, he was tried for sabotage, and he defiantly declared at his trial that freedom was "an ideal for which I am prepared to die." He was given a life sentence.

In the end his death was not required as a price for freedom. In 1990, under mounting international pressure, the South African government released Mandela from prison, where he had suffered for 27 years. In May 1994 he was elected president of a new, free South Africa. This is his inaugural speech.

THE SPEECH

Your Majesties, your Royal Highnesses, distinguished guests, comrades, and friends,

Today, all of us do, by our presence here, and by our celebrations in other parts of our country and the world, confer glory and hope to newborn liberty.

Out of the experience of an extraordinary human disaster that lasted too long, must be born a society of which all humanity will be proud.

Our daily deeds as ordinary South Africans must produce an actual South African reality that will reinforce humanity's belief in justice, strengthen its confidence in the nobility of the human soul, and sustain all our hopes for a glorious life for all. All this we owe both to ourselves and to the peoples of the world who are so well represented here today.

To my compatriots, I have no hesitation in saying that each one of us is as intimately attached to the soil of this beautiful country as are the famous jacaranda trees of Pretoria and the mimosa trees of the bushveld. Each time one of us touches the soil of this land, we feel a sense of personal renewal. The national mood changes as the seasons change. We are moved by a sense of joy and exhilaration when the grass turns green and the flowers bloom.

That spiritual and physical oneness we all share with this common homeland explains the depth of the pain we all carried in our hearts as we saw our country tear itself apart in terrible conflict, and as we saw it spurned, outlawed, and isolated by the peoples of the world, precisely because it has become the universal base of the pernicious ideology and practice of racism and racial oppression.

We, the people of South Africa, feel fulfilled that humanity has taken us back into its bosom, that we, who were outlaws not so long ago, have today been given the rare privilege to be host to the nations of the world on our own soil.

We thank all our distinguished international guests for having come to take possession with the people of our country of what is, after all, a common victory for justice, for peace, for human dignity.

We trust that you will continue to stand by us as we tackle the challenges of building peace, prosperity, non sexism, non racialism, and democracy . . .

The time for the healing of the wounds has come.

The moment to bridge the chasms that divide us has come.

The time to build is upon us.

We have, at last, achieved our political emancipation. We pledge ourselves to liberate all our people from the continuing bondage of poverty, deprivation, suffering, gender and other discrimination.

We succeeded to take our last steps to freedom in conditions of relative peace. We commit ourselves to the construction of a complete, just, and lasting peace.

We have triumphed in the effort to implant hope in the breasts of the millions of our people. We enter into a covenant that we shall build the society in which all South Africans, both black and white, will be able to walk tall, without any fear in their hearts, assured of their inalienable right to human dignity—a rainbow nation at peace with itself and the world . . . We dedicate this day to all the heroes and heroines in this country and the rest of the world who sacrificed in many ways and surrendered their lives so that we could be free.

Their dreams have become reality. Freedom is their reward.

We are both humbled and elevated by the honor and privilege that you, the people of South Africa, have bestowed on us, as the first president of a united, democratic, nonracial, and nonsexist South Africa, to lead our country out of the valley of darkness.

We understand it still that there is no easy road to freedom.

We know it well that none of us acting alone can achieve success.

We must therefore act together as a united people, for national reconciliation, for nation building, for the birth of a new world.

Let there be justice for all. Let there be peace for all. Let there be work, bread, water, and salt for all. Let each know that for each the body, the mind, and the soul have been freed to fulfill themselves.

Never, never, and never again shall it be that this beautiful land will again experience the oppression of one by another and suffer the indignity of being the skunk of the world. The sun shall never set on so glorious a human achievement.

Let freedom reign. God bless Africa.

THE CONSEQUENCES

Defenders of apartheid had long argued that if black South Africans were given the vote, white South Africans would be permanently disenfranchised and a dysfunctional regime would soon put an end to dreams of true democracy.

South Africa's path to freedom was not without dangers, even after the end of apartheid. Much of the populace was desperately poor, angry, and marginalized by decades of discrimination. The hunger for democracy could easily have been overwhelmed by the thirst for revenge.

Fortunately, in Mandela the country had a leader of inspiring vision. In speeches like his inaugural address, he drove the message home that this was a new dawn for all South Africans, not a revolution by some at the expense of others.

Today in the "Rainbow Nation," despite its deeply entrenched social problems, freedom still does reign.

1995

Women's Rights Are Human Rights

Hillary Rodham Clinton

(1947–)

When Hillary Rodham Clinton became the 44th first lady of the United States, the lawyer, advocate, and savvy politico became a different kind of first lady—one who took leadership positions on domestic and international issues.

Born in 1947, Clinton had excelled as a scholar, first at Wellesley and then Yale Law School, where she met her future husband, Bill Clinton. She and Bill were married in 1975 as his political career began in Arkansas. He was elected president of the United States in 1993.

As first lady, Clinton chaired the ultimately unsuccessful Task Force on Health Care Reform, and when she arrived in Beijing as a featured speaker at the United Nation's

Fourth World Conference on Women, there were some who feared that her prominence might damage U.S./China foreign relations. But for Clinton this was an opportunity to "lay down a declaration of American values." The event drew some 50,000 attendees from 180 countries, the largest of its kind.

THE SPEECH

By gathering in Beijing, we are focusing world attention on issues that matter most in the lives of women and their families: access to education, health care, jobs, and credit, the chance to enjoy basic legal and human rights, and to participate fully in the political life of their countries.

There are some who question the reason for this conference. Let them listen to the voices of women in their homes, neighborhoods, and workplaces. There are some who wonder whether the lives of women and girls matter to economic and political progress around the globe. . . .

. . . I believe that, on the eve of a new millennium, it is time to break our silence. It is time for us to say here in Beijing, and the world to hear, that it is no longer acceptable to discuss women's rights as separate from human rights.

These abuses [as Clinton outlined earlier in this speech] have continued because, for too long, the history of women has been a history of silence. Even today, there are those who are trying to silence our words. But the voices of this conference . . . must be heard loudly and clearly:

It is a violation of human rights when babies are denied food, or drowned, or suffocated, or their spines broken, simply because they are born girls.

It is a violation of human rights when women and girls are sold into the slavery of prostitution.

It is a violation of human rights when women are doused with gasoline, set on fire, and burned to death because their marriage dowries are deemed too small.

It is a violation of human rights when individual women are raped in their own communities and when thousands of women are subjected to rape as a tactic or prize of war.

It is a violation of human rights when a leading cause of death worldwide among women ages 14 to 44 is the violence they are subjected to in their own homes.

It is a violation of human rights when young girls are brutalized by the painful and degrading practice of genital mutilation.

It is a violation of human rights when women are denied the right to plan their own families, and that includes being forced to have abortions or being sterilized against their will.

If there is one message that echoes forth from this conference, it is that human rights are women's rights. And women's rights are human rights once and for all.

THE CONSEQUENCES

Many of the assembled delegates—who included high-level representatives, activists, and ordinary women from around the globe—pounded the tables in front of their seats and cheered as Clinton spoke. Her heartfelt yet strident words were in contrast to the more academic, clinical speeches others had given at the conference. Her message, though careful to preserve diplomatic relations, was stinging. Official Chinese news outlets blacked out their coverage.

For Clinton it was a triumph and reinvigorated her sense of purpose. The refrain, "Women's rights are human rights" linked the conference to the emerging international women's rights movement, and for many delegates, hearing the words from the first lady of the United States reassured them that one of the most powerful nations in the world supported their cause.

As secretary of state for President Barack Obama, Hillary Rodham Clinton continued to include the empowerment of women as a key component in global relations and international security.

1996

American Family Values

Christopher Reeve

(1952–2004)

As Christopher Reeve sat alone, dramatically swathed in light on the convention platform, the thousands of attendees at the 1996 Democratic National Convention applauded and cheered. His presence at the convention marked a new role for the 44-year-old actor, director, and activist—as a quadriplegic.

A Juilliard-trained actor, Reeve had first gained fame as Superman in the hugely successful movies of the late 1970s and 1980s. A riding accident in 1995 had paralyzed him, but intensely competitive, Reeve was determined to help find a cure for spinal cord injury. His speech at the convention crystallized a moment in medical research when truly anything seemed possible, and the Democratic Party platform was focused on bringing the nation into the new millennium.

THE SPEECH

Over the last few years, we've heard a lot about something called family values. And like many of you, I've struggled to figure out what that means, but since my accident, I've found a definition that seems to make sense. I think it means that we're all family, that we all have value. . . .

. . . Our nation cannot tolerate discrimination of any kind. That's why the Americans with Disabilities Act is so important, and must be honored everywhere. It is a civil rights law that is tearing down barriers both in architecture and in attitude.

Its purpose is to give the disabled access not only to buildings, but to every opportunity in society. . . .

One of the smartest things we can do about disability is invest in research that will protect us from disease and lead to cures. This country already has a long history of doing just that.

When we put our minds to a problem, we can usually find solutions. But our scientists can do more. And we've got to give them the chance. That means more funding for research. Right now, for example, about a quarter-million Americans have a spinal cord injury.

Our government spends about $8.7 billion a year just maintaining these members of our family. But we spend only $40 million a year on research that would actually improve the quality of their lives, get them off public assistance, or even cure them. We've got to be smarter, do better. Because the money we invest in research today is going to determine the quality of life of members of our family tomorrow.

THE CONSEQUENCES

Reeve's speech cannily played upon the "family values" platform of the Republican Party, admonishing listeners that "You may have an aunt with Parkinson's disease. A neighbor with a spinal cord injury. A brother with AIDS. And if we're really committed to this idea of family, we've got to do something about it." For Reeve this meant expanding funding and support for medical research and initiatives, including controversial stem cell research.

The United States, its policymakers, and major charitable donors were in support of Reeve, and in the years that followed, funding for health research and programs expanded on the federal level, in part due to his consistent lobbying efforts.

Though Reeve resisted acting as spokesperson for the entire disabled community, instead focusing on spinal cord injuries like his own, it was inevitable that the world would see him as a courageous, outspoken advocate for a segment of the population that refused to define itself by its limitations.

2001

Declaration of War on the United States

Osama bin Laden

(1957–2011)

Generous and softly spoken, at least according to those who met him, Osama bin Laden made an unlikely terrorist. The man who has topped the United States's most wanted list for a decade was born into luxury, the seventeenth son of a Yemeni construction magnate living in Saudi Arabia.

But in the 1980s, bin Laden abandoned worldly distractions to fight against Soviet invaders in Afghanistan. Backed by the CIA, among others, he established a camp for Islamic warriors in the border provinces of Pakistan. This camp was simply named "the base," or, in Arabic, Al Qaeda.

The holy war, or jihad, in Afghanistan was a resounding success, and bin Laden sought a new direction for his pious wrath. When U.S. troops established bases on the sacred soil of Saudi Arabia before the first Gulf War of 1991, America presented the perfect target.

Throughout the late 1990s, bin Laden produced a string of violent tirades and fatwas against the American "crusaders." But it was not until 2001, with the devastating 9/11 attack on the World Trade Center in New York, that he found himself with a truly global audience.

THE SPEECH

What the United States tastes today is a very small thing compared to what we have tasted for tens of years. Our nation has been tasting this humiliation and contempt for more than eighty years. Its sons are being killed, its blood is being shed, its holy places are being attacked, and it is not being ruled according to what God has decreed.

Despite this, nobody cares. . . .

One million Iraqi children have thus far died in Iraq although they did not do anything wrong. . . .

Israeli tanks and tracked vehicles also enter to wreak havoc in Palestine, in Jenin, Ramallah, Rafah, Beit Jala, and other Islamic areas and we hear no voices raised or moves made.

But if the sword falls on the United States after eighty years, hypocrisy raises its head lamenting the deaths of these killers who tampered with the blood, honor and holy places of the Muslims.

The least that one can describe these people is that they are morally depraved.

They champion falsehood, support the butcher against the victim, the oppressor against the innocent child.

May God mete them the punishment they deserve. . . .

These incidents divided the entire world into two regions—one of faith where there is no hypocrisy and another of infidelity, from which we hope God will protect us.

The winds of faith and change have blown to remove falsehood from the [Arabian] peninsula of Prophet Mohammad, may God's prayers be upon him.

As for the United States, I tell it and its people these few words: I swear by Almighty God who raised the heavens without pillars that neither the United States nor he who lives in the United States will enjoy security before we can see it as a reality in Palestine and before all the infidel armies leave the land of Mohammad, may God's peace and blessing be upon him.

THE CONSEQUENCES

This message was broadcast on the Arabic news channel Al Jazeera one month after the fall of the Twin Towers. Bin Laden sits cross-legged in a dark cave dressed in a turban and army fatigues, with an AK-47 propped against the rock wall behind him.

The rhetoric is stark. Two weeks earlier U.S. president George W. Bush had said, "Either you are with us, or you are with the terrorists." Bin Laden expressed the same opinion in reverse when he splits the world into "two regions," thus setting the stage for a global confrontation.

Once, his words would have been dismissed as empty threats. But with 9/11, he had proved that he could and would convert word into deed and realize his bloody ambition of an implacable war against the West.

This speech taught the world to believe that it was not dealing with criminals but with holy warriors. The response, therefore, was war—first in Afghanistan, as U.S. and international coalition forces entered Afghanistan with the intent of destroying the Al Qaeda network and overthrowing the ruling Taliban regime, which supported the terrorist group. Two years later troops entered Iraq to root out the perceived threat of weapons of mass destruction, beginning a more than decade-long struggle.

On May 1, 2011, a team of U.S. Navy Seals routed bin Laden from his hiding place in Pakistan, killing him and others in his compound.

2002

The Axis of Evil

George W. Bush

(1946–)

The 9/11 attacks on the World Trade Center in New York in 2001 stunned the United States. For the first time since Pearl Harbor, a foreign enemy had taken American lives on American soil, shattering the comforting illusions of U.S. isolationism.

The response came within a month. United States and British forces invaded Afghanistan and toppled the terrorist-harboring Taliban regime. It was a bold statement of American power—the long arm of international law reaching across continents into Central Asia to pluck out a festering abscess of hostile intent.

Against this backdrop of U.S. force, President George W. Bush prepared to make his 2002 State of the Union address. He was not an exceptional public speaker, better known for blunt certainty than rhetorical sophistication, but this speech proved to be one of American history's defining moments.

THE SPEECH

For many Americans, these four months have brought sorrow, and pain that will never completely go away. Every day a retired firefighter returns to Ground Zero, to feel closer to his two sons who died there. At a memorial in New York, a little boy left his football with a note for his lost father: Dear Daddy, please take this to Heaven. I don't want to play football until I can play with you again some day.

Last month, at the grave of her husband, Michael, a CIA officer and Marine who died in Mazur-e-Sharif, Shannon Spann said these words of farewell: "Semper Fi, my love." Shannon is with us tonight.

Shannon, I assure you and all who have lost a loved one that our cause is just, and our country will never forget the debt we owe Michael and all who gave their lives for freedom.

Our cause is just, and it continues …

What we have found in Afghanistan confirms that, far from ending there, our war against terror is only beginning. Most of the 19 men who hijacked planes on September the 11th were trained in Afghanistan's camps, and so were tens of thousands of others. Thousands of dangerous killers, schooled in the methods of murder, often supported by outlaw regimes, are now spread throughout the world like ticking time bombs, set to go off without warning. . . .

My hope is that all nations will heed our call, and eliminate the terrorist parasites who threaten their countries and our own . . .

But some governments will be timid in the face of terror. And make no mistake about it: If they do not act, America will.

Our . . . goal is to prevent regimes that sponsor terror from threatening America or our friends and allies with weapons of mass destruction. Some of these regimes have been pretty quiet since September the 11th. But we know their true nature. North Korea is a regime arming with missiles and weapons of mass destruction, while starving its citizens.

Iran aggressively pursues these weapons and exports terror, while an unelected few repress the Iranian people's hope for freedom.

Iraq continues to flaunt its hostility toward America and to support terror. The Iraqi regime has plotted to develop anthrax, and nerve gas, and nuclear weapons for over a decade. This is a regime that has already used poison gas to murder thousands of its own citizens—leaving the bodies of mothers huddled over their dead children. This is a regime that agreed to international inspections—then kicked out the inspectors. This is a regime that has something to hide from the civilized world.

States like these, and their terrorist allies, constitute an axis of evil, arming to threaten the peace of the world. By seeking weapons of mass destruction, these regimes pose a grave and growing danger. They could provide these arms to terrorists, giving them the means to match their hatred. They could attack our allies or attempt to blackmail the

> *United States. In any of these cases, the price of indifference would be catastrophic.*
>
> *. . . All nations should know: America will do what is necessary to ensure our nation's security. . . .*
>
> *Our war on terror is well begun, but it is only begun. This campaign may not be finished on our watch—yet it must be and it will be waged on our watch.*

THE CONSEQUENCES

As soon as Bush uttered the words "axis of evil," they started reverberating around the halls of Western power, the almost biblical rhetoric sitting most uneasily with the urbane technocrats of Europe. Chris Patten, the European Union's foreign affairs chief, warned of the dangers of "absolutist positions." The French foreign minister, Hubert Vedrine, cautioned against a new "simplism."

But the speech was a hit with the crowd back home. The wounds of 9/11 still bit deep. Perhaps defeating the Taliban in Afghanistan had seemed almost too easy, and they needed a grand crusade to rid the world of dark forces.

Bush's words laid the foundation for continuing U.S. military involvement in the Middle East. milronically, the campaign that Bush launched with his bellicose address revealed not America's strength but rather the limits of its global reach. Acting unilaterally in the Middle East, the world's most powerful nation found its resources severely and unexpectedly stretched.

2008

Victory Speech

Barack Obama

(1961–)

Barack Obama was an unlikely candidate for the presidency, and even for the Democratic presidential nomination. He was widely considered too young or too inexperienced to hold the highest office. When he announced that he would run in 2007, he was only in his mid-forties and had served a mere two years in the federal government.

And then there was his race. Born in Hawaii to a Kenyan father and a white mother from Kansas, Obama was campaigning to become the first ever African-American president of the United States.

It quickly became clear, however, that he was blessed with a talent for political oratory. In 2004, as a relative unknown, he delivered a keynote speech at the Democratic Convention that catapulted him into the limelight. It had taken him months to prepare—he used to sneak off in the middle of Senate sessions to jot down thoughts—but the effort paid off handsomely. His moving address on the subject of national unity had delegates chanting his name. Out of nowhere he had become a plausible challenger for the Democratic presidential nomination.

Four years and several stirring speeches later, Barack Obama won the presidential election, making history in the process. Addressing a crowd of thousands in Chicago's Grant Park, the soon-to-be-president made his victory speech.

THE SPEECH

If there is anyone out there who still doubts that America is a place where all things are possible; who still wonders if the dream of our founders is alive in our time; who still questions the power of our democracy, tonight is your answer.

It's the answer told by lines that stretched around schools and churches in numbers this nation has never seen; by people who waited three hours and four hours, many for the very first time in their lives, because they believed that this time must be different; that their voice could be that difference.

It's the answer spoken by young and old, rich and poor, Democrat and Republican, black, white, Latino, Asian, Native American, gay, straight, disabled and not disabled—Americans who sent a message to the world that we have never been a collection of Red States and Blue States: We are, and always will be, the United States of America.

It's the answer that led those who have been told for

so long by so many to be cynical, and fearful, and doubtful of what we can achieve to put their hands on the arc of history and bend it once more toward the hope of a better day.

It's been a long time coming, but tonight, because of what we did on this day, in this election, at this defining moment, change has come to America. . . .

The road ahead will be long. Our climb will be steep. We may not get there in one year or even one term, but America—I have never been more hopeful than I am tonight that we will get there. I promise you—we as a people will get there.

There will be setbacks and false starts. There are many who won't agree with every decision or policy I make as president, and we know that government can't solve every problem. But I will always be honest with you about the challenges we face. I will listen to you, especially when we disagree. And above all, I will ask you [to] join in the work of remaking this nation the only way it's been done in America for 221 years—block by block, brick by brick, calloused hand by calloused hand.

What began 21 months ago in the depths of winter must not end on this autumn night. This victory alone is not the change we seek—it is only the chance for us to make that change. And that cannot happen if we go back to the way things were. It cannot happen without you. . . .

And to all those watching tonight from beyond our shores, from parliaments and palaces to those who are huddled around radios in the forgotten corners of our world—our stories are singular, but our destiny is shared, and a new dawn of American leadership is at hand. To those who would tear this world down—we will defeat you.

To those who seek peace and security —we support you. And to all those who have wondered if America's beacon still burns as bright—tonight we proved once more that the true strength of our nation comes not from the might of our arms or the scale of our wealth, but from the enduring power of our ideals: democracy, liberty, opportunity, and unyielding hope.

For that is the true genius of America—that America can change. Our union can be perfected. And what we have already achieved gives us hope for what we can and must achieve tomorrow. . . .

This is our chance to answer that call. This is our moment. This is our tim— to put our people back to work and open doors of opportunity for our kids; to restore prosperity and promote the cause of peace; to reclaim the American Dream and reaffirm that fundamental truth—that out of many, we are one; that while we breathe, we hope, and where we are met with cynicism, and doubt, and those who tell us that we can't, we will respond with that timeless creed that sums up the spirit of a people: Yes We Can.

Thank you, God bless you, and may God bless the United States of America.

THE CONSEQUENCES

For many who watched that day, Obama, with his message of hope and change, looked more like a savior than a politician. In a subsequent poll, more Americans nominated Obama as their "personal hero" than anyone else, including Jesus, Abraham Lincoln, and Mother Teresa.

He was modern, youthful, international. Pundits seized on Obama's Kenyan ancestry and Indonesian upbringing to cast him as a citizen of the world—someone who would end U.S. unilateralism. In 2009 the new president was awarded the Nobel Peace Prize, having been in office for less than a year.

To his critics the Nobel award was a triumph of style over substance. They conceded that Obama was a fine speaker, but at that point, what had he actually done? The Middle Eastern wars remained deadlocked, the outlook gloomy. The economy was floundering. What legislation Obama had pushed through Congress was either considered dangerously progressive (from a right-wing perspective) or tainted by compromise (from the left).

But Obama had shown that he had new ideas and that when he needed to, he could be expert at communicating them. It is too soon to say what the ultimate impact of his presidency may be, but armed with such formidable rhetorical skill, he—and his speeches—may have changed history.

SOURCES

Aung San Suu Kyi. http://thirdworldtraveler.com/Burma/FreedomFrom FearSpeech.html

Ball, John. www.nationalarchives.gov.uk/humanrights

Bin Laden, Osama. http://news.bbc.co.uk/2/hi/south_asia/1585636.stm

Brown, Mark H. www.nezperce.com/npedu11.html

Bush, George W. www.americanrhetoric.com/speeches/ stateoftheunion2002.htm

Churchill, Winston. http://bit.ly/gyYByW

Churchill, Winston. http://bit.ly/eJiYsz

Churchill, Winston. http://bit.ly/9kehYn

Clinton, Hillary Rodham. www.americanrhetoric.com/speeches/ hillaryclintonbeijingspeech.htm

Cromwell, Oliver. www.emersonkent.com/speeches/dismissal_of_the_ rump_parliament.htm

Darrow, Clarence, and William Jennings Bryan. darrow.law.umn.edu/ documents/Scopes%206th%20&%207th%20days.pdf

de Bourrienne, Louis Antoine Fauvelet, ed. by R. W. Phipps. www.gutenberg. org/ratelimiter.php/cache/epub/3563/pg3563.txt

Fisher, Mary. www.maryfisher.org/subjects/whisper-of-aids/whisper-of-aids.htm

Gandhi, Mohandas. www.mkgandhi.org/speeches/bhu.htm

Garibaldi, Guiseppe. www.emersonkent.com/history_notes/giuseppe_ garibaldi.htm#I_offer_hunger,_thirst,_forced_marches,_battles,_and_death

Gehrig, Lou. lougehrig.com/about/speech.htm

Hitler, Adolf. fcit.usf.edu/HOLOCAUST/resource/document/HITLER1.htm

The Holy Bible, Oxford edition. www.kingjamesbibleonline.org/ bookphp?book=Matthew&chapter=5

Homer. www.perseus.tufts.edu/hopper/text?doc=Perseus%3Atext%3A1999.01. 0217%3Abook%3D1%3Acard%3D200

Jordan, Barbara. http://americanradioworks.publicradio.org/features/sayitplain/bjordan.html

Jowett, Benjamin. www.perseus.tufts.edu/hopper/text?doc=Perseus:text:1999.04.0105:book%3D2

Kennedy, John F. www.jfklibrary.org/Asset-Viewer/BqXIEM9F4024ntFl7SVAjA.aspx

Kennedy, John F. www.jfklibrary.org/Research/Ready-Reference/JFK-Speeches/Address-at-Rice-University-on-the-Nations-Space-Effort-September-12-1962.aspx

King, Martin Luther, Jr. www.americanrhetoric.com/speeches/mlkihaveadream.htm

Lenin, Vladimir. http://marxists.org/archive/lenin/works/1917/apr/04.htm

Lincoln, Abraham. www.americanrhetoric.com/speeches/gettysburgaddress.htm

Macmillan, Harold. www.famous-speeches-and-speech-topics.info/famous-speeches/harold-macmillan-speech-wind-of-change.htm

Malcolm X. http://teachingamericanhistory.org/library/index.asp?document=1147

Mandela, Nelson. http://bit.ly/g2kC9f

Mao Zedong. www.international.ucla.edu/eas/documents/mao490921.htm

Munro, Dana Carleton. www.fordham.edu/halsall/source/urban2-5vers.html

Nehru, Jawaharlal. www.guardian.co.uk/theguardian/2007/may/01/greatspeeches

Obama, Barack. http://bit.ly/gvWjLh

Pankhurst, Emmeline. www.guardian.co.uk/theguardian/2007/apr/27/greatspeeches1?INTCMP=ILCNETTXT3487

Reagan, Ronald. www.reaganfoundation.org/pdf/Remarks_on_East_West_Relations_at_Brandenburg%20Gate_061287.pdf

Reeve, Christopher. www.pbs.org/newshour/convention96/floor_speeches/reeve.html

Robespierre, Maximilien. www.historywiz.org/primarysources/justificationterror.htm

Roosevelt, Franklin Delano. http://bit.ly/d7j9DR

Stalin, Joseph. www.ibiblio.org/pha/timeline/411107awp.html

Stanton, Elizabeth Cady, Susan B. Anthony, and Matilda J. Gage, eds. http://historymatters.gmu.edu/d/5740

Thatcher, Margaret. www.margaretthatcher.org

Truth, Sojourner. http://people.sunyulster.edu/VoughtH/sojourner_truth.htm

Vince, J. H. www.perseus.tufts.edu/hopper/text?doc=Perseus:text:1999.01.0070:speech=9:section=68

Washington, George. "www.ourdocuments.gov/doc.php?doc=15&page=transcript

Wilson, Woodrow. www.ourdocuments.gov/doc.php?flash=true&doc=62&page=transcript

Yonge, C. D. www.perseus.tufts.edu/hopper/text?doc=Perseus:text:1999.02.0021:speech%3D13

ACKNOWLEDGMENTS

The author and publishers are grateful to the following for permissions to use material that is in copyright:

Winston Churchill: Reproduced with permission of Curtis Brown Ltd, London on behalf of the Estate of Sir Winston Churchill: Copyright © Winston S. Churchill.

Nelson Mandela: Extracts reproduced with permission from the Nelson Mandela Foundation.

Martin Luther King, Jr.: Reprinted by arrangement with The Heirs to the Estate of Martin Luther King Jr., c/o Writers House as agent for the proprietor, New York, NY. Copyright 1962 Dr. Martin Luther King Jr.; copyright renewed 1991 Coretta Scott King.

INDEX OF FAMOUS LINES

A

"All nations should know: America will do what is necessary to ensure our nation's security. . . ." ***George W. Bush,*** 158

"And aren't I a woman? Look at me! Look at my arm! I have plowed and planted and gathered into barns, and no man could head me!" ***Sojourner Truth,*** 43

"A new star rises, the star of freedom in the east, a new hope comes into being, a vision long cherished materializes. May the star never set and that hope never be betrayed!" ***Jawaharlal Nehru,*** 95–96

"Ask not what your country can do for you—ask what you can do for your country." ***John F. Kennedy,*** 109

B

"Blessed are the meek: for they shall inherit the earth." ***Jesus of Nazareth,*** 20

"But we will put the enemy in the position where they will have to choose between giving us freedom or giving us death." ***Emmeline Pankhurst,*** 55

E

"Either you are with us, or you are with the terrorists." ***George W. Bush***, 153

F

"For even if all other states succumb to slavery, we surely must fight the battle of liberty." ***Demonsthenes,*** 16

"For the whole earth is the sepulchre of famous men . . ." ***Pericles,*** 15

"Fourscore and seven years ago our fathers brought forth on this continent a new nation . . ." ***Abraham Lincoln,*** 47

"From where the sun now stands, I will fight no more forever." ***Chief Joseph,*** 51

G

"Go, get you out! Make haste! Ye venal slaves be gone!" ***Oliver Cromwell,*** 29

"Undertake this journey for the remission of your sins, with the assurance of the imperishable glory of the kingdom of heaven. . . ." ***Pope Urban II,*** 25

I

"I am from now on just first soldier of the German Reich. I have once more put on that coat. . . . I will not take it off again until victory is secured, or I will not survive the outcome. . . ." ***Adolf Hitler,*** 74

"I am here as a soldier who has temporarily left the field of battle . . ." ***Emmeline Pankhurst,*** 54

"I believe it is peace for our time." ***Neville Chamberlain,*** 76

"If there is anyone out there who still doubts that America is a place where all things are possible . . . tonight is your answer." ***Barack Obama,*** 160

"If there is one message that echoes forth from this conference, it is that human rights are women's rights." ***Hillary Rodham Clinton,*** 146

"If the spring of popular government in time of peace is virtue, the springs of popular government in revolution are at once virtue and terror: virtue, without which terror is fatal; terror, without which virtue is powerless." ***Maximilien Robespierre,*** 33

"If the white people realize what the alternative is, perhaps they will be more willing to hear Dr. King." ***Malcolm X,*** 117

"If we don't do something real soon, I think you'll have to agree that we're going to be forced either to use the ballot or the bullet." ***Malcolm X,*** 117

"I have a dream that my four little children will one day live in a nation where they will not be judged by the color of their skin but by the content of their character." ***Martin Luther King. Jr.,*** 113

"I have already intimated to you the danger of parties in the State, with particular reference to the founding of them on geographical discrimination." ***George Washington,*** 36

"I have nothing to offer but blood, toil, tears, and sweat." ***Winston Churchill,*** 78

"I have sacrificed all of my interests to those of the country. I go, but you, my friends, will continue to serve France. Her happiness was my only thought. It will still be the object of my wishes." ***Napoleon Bonaparte,*** 39

"Inflation destroys nations and societies as surely as invading armies do." ***Margaret Thatcher,*** 124

"It is not power that corrupts but fear. Fear of losing power corrupts those who wield it and fear of the scourge of power corrupts those who are subject to it. . . ." ***Aung San Suu Kyi,*** 133

"It is reason, and not passion, which must guide our deliberations, guide our debate, and guide our decision." ***James Madison,*** 121

"It's been a long time coming, but tonight, because of what we did on this day, in this election, at this defining moment, change has come to America. . . ." ***Barack Obama,*** 161

"I want you to know tonight, that we, as a people, will get to the Promised Land." ***Martin Luther King, Jr.,*** 116

"I want the world to know that this man, who does not believe in a God, is trying to use a court in Tennessee . . . to slur at it, and, while it require time, I am willing to take it." ***William Jennings Bryan,*** 67

J

"Just and amicable feelings towards all [nations] should be cultivated. The nation which indulges towards another an habitual hatred, or an habitual fondness, is in some degree a slave. . . ." ***George Washington,*** 36

L

"Let every nation know, whether it wishes us well or ill, that we shall pay any price, bear any burden, meet any hardship, support any friend, oppose any foe to assure the survival and the success of liberty . . ." ***John F. Kennedy,***

108
"Let freedom reign. God bless Africa." ***Nelson Mandela,*** 143
"Let the word go forth from this time and place, to friend and foe alike, that the torch has been passed to a new generation of Americans. . . ." ***John F. Kennedy,*** 107
"Let us therefore brace ourselves to our duties, and so bear ourselves that, if the British Empire and its Commonwealth last for a thousand years, men will still say, 'This was their finest hour.'" ***Winston Churchill,*** 81
"Liberty, Equality, Fraternity." ***French Republic motto,*** 41
"Long years ago we made a tryst with destiny . . ." ***Jawaharlal Nehru,*** 95

M

"Mr. Gorbachev, tear down this wall! . . ." ***Ronald Reagan,*** 130

N

"Never, never, and never again shall it be that this beautiful land will again experience the oppression of one by another." ***Nelson Mandela,*** 143
"No matter how long it may take us to overcome this premeditated invasion, the American people in their righteous might will win through to absolute victory." ***Franklin D. Roosevelt,*** 91–92

O

"Our Father which art in heaven, Hallowed be thy name." ***Jesus of Nazareth,*** 21
"Ours will no longer be a nation subject to insult and humiliation. We have stood up. . . ." ***Mao Zedong,*** 99
"Over the last few years, we've heard a lot about something called family values. And like many of you, I've struggled to figure out what that means. . . . I think it means that we're all family, that we all have value." ***Christopher Reeve,*** 149

P

"Political power grows out of the barrel of a gun." ***Mao Zedong,*** 101

R

"Revolution is bloody." ***Malcolm X,*** 116

S

"So I close in saying that I might have been given a bad break, but I've got an awful lot to live for." ***Lou Gehrig,*** 70
"I offer neither pay, nor quarters, nor provisions. I offer hunger, thirst, forced marches, battles and death. Let him who loves his country follow me." ***Guiseppe Garibaldi,*** 82
"States like these, and their terrorist allies, constitute an axis of evil. . . . By seeking weapons of mass destruction, these regimes pose a grave and growing danger." ***George W. Bush,*** 157

T

"That's one small step for man. One giant leap for mankind." ***Neil Armstrong,*** 110
"The Chinese people, comprising one quarter of humanity, have now stood up." ***Mao Zedong,*** 99
"The devil is not as terrible as he is painted." ***Joseph Stalin,*** 86

"The Eagle has landed."
Neil Armstrong, 110
"The masses must be made to see that the Soviets of Workers' Deputies are the only possible form of revolutionary government . . ."
Vladimir Lenin, 88
"[The people of the United States] are ready to put their own strength, their own highest purpose, their own integrity and devotion to the test."
Woodrow Wilson, 63
"There is no salvation for India unless you strip yourselves of this jewelry and hold it in trust for your countrymen in India."
Mahatma Gandhi, 58–59
"These incidents divided the entire world into two regions—one of faith where there is no hypocrisy and another of infidelity, from which we hope God will protect us." ***Osama bin Laden,*** 153
"The time for the healing of the wounds has come. The moment to bridge the chasms that divide us has come." ***Nelson Mandela,*** 141
"The wind of change is blowing through this continent, and whether we like it or not, this growth of national consciousness is a political fact."
Harold Macmillan, 103
"Though seas and mountains, and vast regions lay between you, still you would hate such a man without seeing him." ***Cicero,*** 17
"Today I am an inquisitor. . . . My faith in the Constitution is whole, it is complete, it is total."
Barbara Jordan, 119

W

"We choose to go to the moon . . . not because [it is] easy, but because [it is] hard."
John F. Kennedy, 110
"We hold these truths to be self-evident, that all men are created equal . . ."
Declaration of Independence, 49
"We knew the world would not be the same. A few people laughed, a few people cried, most people were silent. I remembered the line from the Hindu scripture, the Bhagavad-Gita: 'Now, I am become Death, the destroyer of worlds.'"
J. Robert Oppenheimer, 93
"We shall fight on the beaches, we shall fight on the landing grounds, we shall fight in the fields and in the streets, we shall fight in the hills; we shall never surrender,"
Winston Churchill, 80
"When Adam delved and Eve span, who was then the gentleman?"
John Ball, 30
"Wine-bibber . . . with the face of a dog and the heart of a hind, you never dare to go out with the host in fight, nor yet with our chosen men in ambuscade. You shun this as you do death itself."
Homer, 14
"With this faith, we will be able to hew out of the mountain of despair a stone of hope."
Martin Luther King, Jr., 114

Y

"Ye are a pack of mercenary wretches, and would like Esau sell your country for a mess of pottage, and like Judas betray

your God for a few pieces of money." ***Oliver Cromwell,*** 28
"Yes, across Europe, this wall will fall. For it cannot withstand faith; it cannot withstand truth. The wall cannot withstand freedom." ***Ronald Reagan,*** 130
"Yesterday, December 7, 1941—a date which will live in infamy—the United States of America was suddenly and deliberately attacked by naval and air forces of the Empire of Japan." ***Franklin D. Roosevelt,*** 90
"You are HIV positive, but dare not say it. You have lost loved ones, but you dare not whisper the word AIDS." ***Mary Fisher,*** 137
"You turn if you want to. The lady's not for turning." ***Margaret Thatcher,*** 126

GENERAL INDEX

A

Achilles, 14
adultery, 20–21
Afghanistan
  G.W. Bush on, 156
  Soviet invasion, 151
  US in, 154, 155, 158
Africa, 102–105
African Americans
  Barbara Jordan, 118–122
  Malcolm X, 116–117
  Martin Luther King, Jr., 111–116
  Sojourner Truth, 42–45
AIDS, 136–138
ALS (amyotrophic lateral sclerosis), 71
American Civil War, 46–48
"American Family Values" (Reeve), 148–150
American Indians, 50–52
Americans with Disabilities Act, 149
amyotrophic lateral sclerosis (ALS), 71
ancient Greece, 13–16
ancient Rome, 17–18
apartheid, 103, 105, 139, 143. *See also racism*
"April Theses" (Lenin), 88
Aristotle, 13–14
Armstrong, Neil, 110
"Aren't I a Woman?" (Truth), 42–45
assassinations
  Abraham Lincoln, 49
  John F. Kennedy, 110
  Martin Luther King, Jr., 116
Athens, ancient, 15–16
atom bomb, 93
Aung San Suu Kyi, 132–135
"Axis of Evil" (Bush), 155–158

B

Ball, John, 30
baseball, farewell to, 69–71
Bay of Pigs invasion, 109
Berlin Wall, 109, 127–131
bin Laden, Osama, 151–154
"Blood, Toil, Tears and Sweat" (Churchill), 78–79, 82
Bolsheviks, 83–84, 87
Booth, John Wilkes, 49
Britain, Battle of, 80, 81
British Empire. *See also United Kingdom*
  English Civil War, 27
  in India, 57–60, 94–97
  monarchy, 30
Bryan, William Jennings, 65–68

Burma (Myanmar), 132–135
Bush, George W., 153, 155–158
Byzantine Empire, 23–24

C

Chamberlain, Neville, 76
Charles I (King of England), 27
Charles II (King of England), 30
Chief Joseph, 50–52
China, 98–101
"Chinese People Have Stood Up" (Mao Zedong), 98–101
Christianity
  Crusades, 23–26
  Scopes Trial and, 65–68
  Sermon on the Mount, 19–22
Churchill, Winston
  background, 77–78
  "Blood, Toil, Tears and Sweat," 78–79, 82
  consequences, 81
  "Finest Hour," 80–81
  "We Shall Fight on the Beaches," 79–80
Cicero, 17
Civil Rights Act, 115
civil rights movements
  Mahatma Gandhi, 57
  Malcolm X, 116–117
  Martin Luther King, Jr., 111–116
civil wars
  American Civil War, 46–48
  English Civil War, 27
classical orations
  background, 13–14
  Cicero, 17
  consequences, 18
  Demosthenes, 16
  Homer, 14
  Pericles, 15
classism, 30
Clinton, Hillary Rodham, 144–147
communism collapse, 131
Constantine the Great, 22
Constantinople, 23
Council of Clermont, 23–26
Cromwell, Oliver, 27–30
Crusades, 23–26
Cuban missile crisis, 109–110
Czechoslovakia, 76, 78

D

Darrow, Clarence, 65–68
"Date Which Will Live in Infamy" (Roosevelt), 89–93
Declaration of Independence, 49
Declaration of war on United States (bin Laden), 151–154
Demonsthenes, 16
Depayin Massacre, 135
divorce, 21

E

Emancipation Proclamation, 45, 111
English Civil War, 27
evolution, teaching of, 65–68

F

farewell addresses
  George Washington, 35–37
  Lou Gehrig, 69–71
  Napoleon Bonaparte, 38–40
feminism. *See women's rights*
"Finest Hour" (Churchill), 80–81
"First Soldier of the German Reich" (Hitler), 72–75
Fisher, Mary, 136–138
foreign policy
  George Washington on, 36–37
  Woodrow Wilson on, 61–64
"Fourteen Points" (Wilson), 61–64
France
  French Revolution, 31–34, 38, 41
  motto, 41
  World War II, 75, 78
France, Battle of, 78
"Freedom From Fear" (Aung San Suu Kyi), 132–135
"Freedom or Death" (Pankhurst), 53–56
Funeral oration (Pericles), 15

G

Gage, Frances, 43–45
Gandhi, Mahatma, 57–60
Garibaldi, Guisepee, 82
Gehrig, Lou, 69–71
geographic regionalism, 36, 37
Germany
  Berlin Wall, 109, 127–131
  World War II, 75, 84–87
Gettysburg Address, 46–49
Gospels, 19–20
Greece, ancient, 13–16

H

Hardinge, Charles, 59
Henry, Patrick, 55
Hiroshima bombing, 93
Hitler, Adolf, 72–75, 76, 78
HIV/AIDS, 136–138
Holocaust, 75
Homer, 14
Hurd, Douglas, 104

I

"I Have a Dream" (King), 111–116
Iliad, The (Homer), 14
inaugural addresses
  John F. Kennedy, 107–109
  Nelson Mandela, 140–143
India, independence of, 58–60, 94–97
Iraq, 154, 157
Italy, 82
"I Will Fight No More Forever" (Chief Joseph), 50–52

J

Jacobin Club, 31–34
Japan, 89–93
Jefferson, Thomas, 49
Jerusalem, 26
Jesus of Nazareth, 19–22
Jordan, Barbara
  background, 118–119
  consequences, 122
  "Today I Am an Inquisitor," 119–121
Joseph (Chief of Nez Percé), 50–52

K

Kennedy, John F.
  assassination, 110
  background, 106–107
  consequences, 109–110
  inaugural address, 107–109
  space exploration pledge, 110
Khruschev, Nikita, 109–110
King, Martin Luther Jr.
  assassination, 116
  background, 111–112
  consequences, 115–116
  "I Have a Dream," 112–115

L

"Lady's Not for Turning" (Thatcher), 123–126
League of Nations, 64
Lenin, Vladimir, 84, 88
"Let Freedom Reign" (Mandela), 139–143
Liberty, Equality, Fraternity, 41
Lincoln, Abraham
  assassination, 49
  background, 46–47
  consequences, 48–49
  Emancipation Proclamation, 45, 111
  Gettysburg Address, 47–48
Lou Gehrig's Disease, 71
lunar landing, 110

M

Macmillan, Harold, 102–105
Madison, James, 121
Malcolm X, 116–117
Mandela, Nelson
  background, 139–140
  consequences, 143
  inaugural speech, 140–143
Mao Zedong, 98–101

Mark Antony, 17
Matthew, Gospel of, 20–21
Midway, Battle of, 92–93
moon walk, 110
Mountbatten, Louis, 94
Myanmar (Burma), 132–135

N

Nagasaki bombing, 93
Napoleon Bonaparte, 38–40
Napoleonic Wars, 38–40
Nation of Islam, 116
Nazi regime, 73, 78
Nehru, Jawaharlal, 94–97
Nero, 22
Nez Percé, 50–52
Nixon, Richard, 118–122
Nobel Peace Prize, 133, 163
nonviolent resistance, 57
"No Salvation for India" (Gandhi), 57–60

O

Obama, Barack
 background, 159–160
 consequences, 162–163
 Nobel Peace Prize, 163
 victory speech, 160–162
October Revolution, 87
October Revolution anniversary speech (Stalin), 83–87
Old Guard, farewell to, 38–40
Oppenheimer, J. Robert, 93
Oswald, Lee Harvey, 110

P

Pakistan, 97
Pankhurst, Emmeline, 53–56
Parliament of Saints, 27, 29
partisanship, 36, 37
Patten, Chris, 158
peace, 61–64
Pearl Harbor attack
 background, 89–90
 consequences, 92–93
 "Date Which Will Live in Infamy," 90–92
Peasant's Revolt, 30
Peloponnesian War, 15
Pericles, 15
Philip II of Macedon, 16
Philippics (Cicero), 17
Philippics (Demonsthenes), 16
Poland, 73–75, 78
political parties, 36, 37

R

racism and discrimination
 American, 111–112, 115–116
 South African, 103, 105, 139, 143
Reagan, Ronald
 background, 127–128
 consequences, 131
 "Tear Down This Wall!", 128–130
Reeve, Christopher, 148–150
Reign of Terror, 31–34
Religion. *See Christianity*
rhetoric, 13–14
Robert the Monk, 24–25
Robespierre, Maximilien, 31–34
Rome, ancient, 17–18
Roosevelt, Franklin Delano, 89–93
Rump Parliament, 27–30

S

satyagraha, 57
Scopes Trial, 65–68
September 11, 2001
 bin Laden response, 151–154
 G. W. Bush response, 155–158
Sermon on the Mount, 19–22
Sharpeville Massacre, 139
slavery
 Civil War, 46–48
 Sojourner Truth and, 42–45
South Africa
 Harold Macmillan, 102–105
 Mahatma Gandi, 57
 Nelson Mandela, 139–143

Soviet Union
communism collapse, 131
October Revolution, 87
World War I, 88
World War II, 75, 84–87
space exploration, 110
spinal cord injuries, 148–150
Stalin, Joseph
background, 83–84
consequences, 87
October Revolution anniversary speech, 84–86
stem cell research, 150
Stowe, Harriet Beecher, 44
Sudtenland, 76
suffragettes, 53–56

T

"Tear Down This Wall!" (Reagan), 128–130
Terror, The (French Revolution), 31–34
terrorism. See September 11, 2001
Thatcher, Margaret, 123–126
Third Philippic (Demonsthenes), 16
Third Reich, 73
Thirteenth Philippic (Cicero), 17
"Today I Am an Inquisitor" (Jordan), 118–122
Truth, Sojourner, 42–45
"Tryst with Destiny" (Nehru), 94–97

U

United Kingdom, 75, 80–81. *See also British Empire*
United States of America
in Afghanistan, 154, 155, 158
Civil War, 46–48
Declaration of Independence, 49
declaration of war on (2001), 151–154
foreign policy, 36–37, 61–64
Indian Wars, 50–52
World War I, 61–64
World War II, 75, 89–93
Urban II (pope), 23–26

V

Vedrine, Hubert, 158
Versailles, Treaty of, 64
victory speech (Obama), 159–163
Voting Rights Act, 115, 117

W

Washington, George, 35–37
Watergate scandal, 118–122
Waterloo, Battle of, 40
Wellington, Duke of, 40
"We Shall Fight on the Beaches" (Churchill), 79–80
"Whisper of AIDS" (Fisher), 136–138
Wilson, Woodrow, 61–64
"Wind of Change" (Macmillan), 102–105
Winter Campaign, 87
women's rights
Emmeline Pankhurst, 53–56
Hillary Rodham Clinton, 144–147
Sojourner Truth, 42–45
"Women's Rights Are Human Rights" (Clinton), 144–147
Women's Social and Political Union (WSPU), 53–54
World Trade Center. *See September 11, 2001*
World War I
Vladimir Lenin, 88
Wilson's fourteen points, 61–64
World War II
Adolf Hitler, 72–75, 76, 78
Franklin Roosevelt, 89–93
Joseph Stalin, 84–87
Winston Churchill, 77–81
WSPU, 53–54

delivered at the dedication of the

o Gettysburg.

and seven years ago our fathers

rth on this continent, a new na

ived in Liberty, and dedicated

position that all men are cre

e.

are engaged in a great civil war

ether that nation, or any nation

ed and so dedicated, can long

We are met on a great battle fie

r. We have come to dedicate a

f that field, as a final resting

those who here gave their lives

nation might live. It is alto

tting and proper that we should